PLAY.
SPEAK.

Tia Dionne Hodge-Jones

40 Monologues
for young actors

First Printing 2014

Print: 978-0-9797868-8-4
eBook: 978-0-9915961-0-2

DEDICATION

For Mirsada & My Logan
And to every performer that has the courage to step out
into the dream and dare the curtain to rise.

CONTENTS

ACKNOWLEDGEMENTS

I am truly and deeply blessed to be able to do what I do, and to be able to work and play with the many amazing people I have had the opportunity to know. I thank God and everyone that has contributed to the many voices that are not only a part of this collection, but a part of my life and heart.

I would especially like to thank:

My husband, Thomas, for being the love of my life, my loudest cheerleader, and the first editor of this collection. Thank you for putting in so many long hours organizing the pieces and pushing me to finally put them all together

My parents—Susan and Edward, and my sisters—Tiffany and Tanya—and all of my family for their unconditional love, support and laughter

My dear friends, Howard, Dean and Liz Kravitz, and all the faculty, staff, students and parents at Performers Theatre Workshop for their years of encouragement and trust in my work. Thank you for inspiring me to truly listen to the voices that bubble up from your very spirits

Darrell Gunter for his wisdom, guidance and help in pushing this book forward

Jane Mandel and Frankie Faison for their friendship, support and never-ending mentorship

Professor Shanna Beth McGee for teaching me how to write a monologue with action and conflict, and Professor Catherine Albers for guiding me in the dream to perform

Dr. Daniel Dyer and Dr. Norman Fischer for inspiring me so many years ago

David Hansen for challenging me and "The Swing Poets of Theatre"—Dan Kilbane, Trishalana Kopaitich, Keith Lukianowicz, Charles Ogg and Sarah Morton—to write monologues and scenes for *Bummer* at Dobama Theatre's Night Kitchen. You opened the door to so much more than just a few nights of pure joy on stage

Cheryl Ann Kennedy, Gwendolyn Steele, and Karen Timmerman for their sisterhood and guidance

Sarah Morton for your beauty and creative genius that challenges me to hold on even when the pressure of creating gets rough

INTRODUCTION

Why another collection of monologues for young actors?

In 2000, I began working as an acting instructor for Performers Theatre Workshop (Maplewood, NJ). My students ranged in ages from 3-years-old to 44—from babies with print agents, nationally running commercials and TV shows, to tweens and teens preparing for school forensics competitions, college, and agent/manager auditions, to moms and dads looking for a new form of self-expression and career opportunities—I had them all. The majority of them, however, were young actors eager to have fun. For that group, my job was (and still is) to introduce them to character study, scene study, and audition technique. All I had to do was have my students fall in love with the process of becoming someone else in a given circumstance and believe without fear that that process would carry them, and give them the courage to *play* and *speak* as another person. Yeah! Well... (Beat) Humph! You try telling an 8-year-old that the piece she has brought in isn't stretching her enough, and NOT get a weird look. Or, try to get a 15-year-old boy to find a piece that will get him in touch with his fear or rage, and NOT have it take him three weeks to do it? I'm not saying it can't be done. Hey, I know it can! However, I only have one hour per week for ten weeks to make it all come together, and with their schedules—homework, sports commitments, part-time jobs, auditions, family and other responsibilities—and mine... Yes, I'm a professional actor, wife, and mother here, people! I found myself fighting an uphill battle with just my students getting material that would fit, stretch and interest them. So... (Beat) Yup, that's right! You guessed it. I started writing for them. Heck, who has the time to argue about a piece when you've got one written for you?! Ha-ha! Not me! And, NOT my students. They began to get excited about each new piece, and some even began collecting many of them themselves. To this day, I have students that come back to visit and tell me how they remember the first monologue I had written for them, and how it got them that agent/manager, or (my favorite) how it made them feel special because someone took the time to really see their strengths and weaknesses, and channeled them into a piece that took their acting to another level. Wow. Now that's what it's all about. Truly. And, that's what this collection is about. It's about voices. It's about young people. It's about the voices of young people moving beyond the four walls of my classroom and sharing those voices with the many out there. (Beat) If you are a young actor, all I ask is that you dig deep, look beyond the words on the page and challenge yourself to see past the obvious description of the characters outlined in each piece. Look for the parts of yourself that connect you to the character, and then go even farther. And, if you are an instructor, I ask that you encourage your students to redefine what acting is for themselves. Is it in the pretending? Is it in the breath, the physical nature of the character, the taking on of said circumstances, or is it the letting go of self and falling head first into the unknown and coming out the other end as a truly and fully realized new being that is them and not them all at once? Ooo... (Beat) Can you feel me? I mean, can you really feel me, my people?! I hope you can. I truly hope so because now it's up to you to take these pieces and make them your own. I know you can do it. And, I know you can take your acting to the next level and beyond... All you have to do is believe. (Beat) Ok, read and believe. (Beat) No, really. Read the next section—Breaking It Down—so you can understand how to easily break down a monologue, and then? Go read the monologues. Note that within each section, the monologues increase in character complexity, but there are no ages or age ranges associated with each monologue. Why? Well, in my experience, the voice of each character is not always limited by the age of the young actor taking it on, but only by the level of his or her commitment to the work. So...(Beat) Really... Go read the next section, do what it explains, and challenge yourself to take on becoming someone. Then read the monologues... And then? Believe. (Beat) NOW!

PLAY. SPEAK.

BREAKING IT DOWN

It's the Who, Whom, When, Where, What, Why, How, What and How again, Right?

So... You want to break down a monologue? You want to understand the character you're playing and get to the good stuff? Well, my friend, you're going to have to ask yourself a few simple questions. That's right. You're going to have to ask some questions and then answer them, and then ask a few more questions and then answer those. Yeah, yeah... I know, I know. You're thinking, questions-squestions! Who has time for that? (By the way, that was a question. Duh!) Anyway... Your job as an actor is to ask the questions that will give you the answers to unlocking the character you're playing. Why? (Uh, that's another question. Just thought you should know.) BECAUSE! Answering these questions will give you a roadmap into the world of the person you are to become, and THAT is worth its weight in gold. How much gold? Who knows? But I like gold, so... Let's try this thing out shall we? OK!

1. READ THE MONOLOGUE! (The whole thing. No cheating!)

Example Monologue: Troop 666

(Megan and her Girl Scout troop are going to collect their cookie money, and they don't take "No" for an answer. Ever.)

Megan: Hi Mrs. Malcowitzky. Hi. Yes, I know you're sitting shiva... But it's Tuesday, and like you said, Tuesday after 4 but not after 5 would be the best time to stop by. So, here we are. 4:02 on the dot, and I hope we can settle things. (Beat) Yes, I can see that, Mrs. Malcowitzky. So sad. Everyone in black... We are all so very sorry to hear of Mr. Malcowitzky's passing. He was a wonderful man. A legend really. There's not a kid in the neighborhood that doesn't know how he single-handedly tried to save little Kelly Steven's cat. (Choking up) In the corner of my mind, I can still see him... Up there, all alone in that big sycamore tree, literally out on a limb for a cat named Spuds. It was like watching a miracle to see him scamper his, what, 375 pound frame up that tree in like 10 seconds—he was like Spider-Man! And then reach out his fat, fleshy fingers, pull Spuds to him and hold that cat like a newborn babe. A true hero. And to honor him, you see here? I've immortalized him with a new stripe on my sash. I embroidered it myself. If you look close, you can even see his smile and his hands around Spuds... before he fell and crushed him, of course. Yeah. It's not standard GS—that's Girl Scouts—but I got permission to put it on there because of his heroics and, well, because he was such a loyal and faithful customer. As you know, every year he almost single-handedly sends us—Troop 666—to the national convention. So... I would hope that, even in death, he would continue to honor his commitments and pay up for all the Do-Si-Dos, Lemonades, Reduced Fat Daisy Go Rounds, and Tagalongs he ordered before his untimely demise. (Beat) Mrs. Malcowitzky, we know he ordered them... All your guests are eating Thin Mints! (Beat) Do you want a scene, or do I need to call in more troops? (Beat) Yes, we take checks.

2. Ok, so you've read the monologue, and now it's time to ask yourself some questions. But before you do, I want to ask if you noticed the word "Beat" in parentheses? And, if you did—and I sure hope you did—you'll need to know what it means. Simply, it means to take a short pause. It is also a valuable clue that you can use to help break down a monologue. We'll get to that soon enough, but I want you to be aware of such a great clue, and keep it in the back of your mind.

3. Alright! So now it's time to ask yourself the first question: "WHO AM I?" That's correct, "I". Not who is she (or he), not who is this character, but WHO AM I? You're playing the part, you are embodying this person and giving her a heartbeat, so you must address the question in the first person. In this case, you would answer the question by stating: I am Megan. Simple, right?

4. Now ask, "TO WHOM AM I SPEAKING?" I know you want to say, "Well, it's a monologue, so I must be speaking to the audience." Well, no. As the actor you may be "playing toward" the audience, but as a fully realized character, you'd actually be speaking to a specific person. So, what is the answer to this question? The answer is: I am speaking to Mrs. Malcowitzky.

5. Next, ask yourself, "WHEN IS THIS TAKING PLACE?" Easy right? Is the character you're playing living in present day, or the 1950s? Is the time even more specific? Is it exactly 12PM or is it 12AM? Knowing the "when" will give you insight into the character's way of being because how one would behave at 12PM may be quite different than at 12AM, and knowing the way in which people behaved in certain situations in the present may be very different than how people behaved in the 1950s. Also, don't forget the seasons, the month of the year, or the weather! These too are very important because they will reflect in how you approach your character. Always look for clues that would help you place the "when". Using our example monologue, you will find that as Megan you say, "Hi. Yes, I know you're sitting shiva... But it's Tuesday, and like you said, Tuesday after 4 but not after 5 would be the best time to stop by. So, here we are. 4:02 on the dot, and I hope we can settle things." The first thing that pops out is "sitting shiva". To "sit shiva" is a mourning ritual practiced in the Jewish faith after a family member or other loved one has passed away. In this case, Mr. Malcowitzky has died, and his wife and her guests are mourning him. Therefore, part of the "when" is while Mrs. Malcowiztky is mourning the death of her husband. Also, it is Tuesday at 4:02, and it's probably the afternoon because 4:02 in the morning would be too early for little girls to be walking the streets. It's up to you to be as specific as you'd like as long as it helps to

narrow you in on how the "when" affects your character's behavior. Let's keep it simple and answer the question like this: This moment is taking place in the present, on a sunny Tuesday at 4:02PM, while Mrs. Malcowitzky and her guests are mourning the death of Mr. Malcowitzky.

6. It's time to ask, "WHERE IS THIS TAKING PLACE?" Again, an easy and specific question to answer now that you've placed the "when". Using our example, you would answer this question by stating, "I'm standing at the door of Mrs. Malcowitzky house." (Oo! It's getting fun, right?)

7. Now for the good stuff. Ask yourself, "WHAT DO I WANT?" In this moment and under these circumstances, WHAT DO I WANT? This is very important because this is the reason you're speaking in the first place. This is the fuel for the fire that IS the monologue. If you didn't really want anything then it wouldn't be a monologue, it would be just silence, but it IS a monologue and you have something to say BECAUSE you WANT something. Now, as the character, you may not get what you want, but at the very least you set out to get it. So, make sure your answer to this is very simple and clear. The more simple and the more clear, the better. To use our "Troop 666" example, as Megan you say, "As you know, every year he almost single-handedly sends us—Troupe 666—to the national convention. So... I would hope that, even in death, he would continue to honor his commitments and pay up for all the

Do-Si-Dos, Lemonades, Reduced Fat Daisy Go Rounds, and Tagalongs he ordered before his untimely demise." You may be tempted to answer the question of "what do I want" like this: "I want Mrs. Malcowitzky to give me the money her deceased husband owes me." Or, to be even more simple, you could say: "I want my money!" It's simple and clear.

8. Next, ask "WHY DO I WANT WHAT I WANT?" Again, make sure your answer is simple and clear. In this case, there is a reason why you want the money. And, the REASON you want the money is the true answer to our question. You want the money BECAUSE you want to go to the national convention. Therefore, the answer to the question of "why do I want what I want" would be as follows: I want my money so my troop and I can go to the Girl Scout's national convention. Got it? Good!

9. Now, ask yourself "HOW WILL I GET WHAT I WANT?" This is very important. You see, in pursuing what you want you need to know how you will actively be going after it, and that makes all the difference. Actively pursuing what you want and choosing an action on either each line or phrase brings the piece to life. For example, in one moment you will butter her up, while in the next chastise her, or plead, and then threaten her in the next. Also, remember when I asked you if you noticed the word "Beat" in parentheses, and that it meant to take a short pause? Well, the term "beat" is also a unit of action—a phrase, breath, internal idea, or momentum that changes—and was first

introduced by the great, Constantin Stanislavski, whom many have considered to be the "Father of Modern Acting". Simply, it's when the actor changes gears from moment-to-moment—beat-to-beat—and it is this that helps build a fully realized piece of acting. Later, Step 11 will show you how to map and use beats, but for now, know that each beat reflects back to why you want what you want and how you're going to get it. In reference to our example monologue again, you want to go to the national convention.

10. Ask yourself, "WHAT HAPPENED JUST BEFORE THIS MOMENT THAT WOULD HAVE ME SPEAK RIGHT NOW?" Something must have happened that would make you want to take action and actually speak now. Why? Because, again, it's a monologue, and if nothing happened before you speak, then what's the big deal? In this example monologue, we can conclude that you had spoken to Mrs. Malcowitztky sometime earlier the week before, and she had told you to come by her home on Tuesday. We can also imagine that you and your troop were out collecting money from your cookie sales, and just before this moment you saw people visiting Mrs. Malcowitzy's house, and many of them were eating your Girl Scout cookies. What we want to focus on is how seeing this is affecting you. How is this moment—the moment you see her guests eating those unpaid for Thin Mints—affecting your way of being? Are you disappointed? Are you saddened, angry, or annoyed? However you choose to imagine the moment, use

that to propel you into the monologue, as this way of being helps to establish how and why you are behaving the way you are and speaking to Mrs. Malcowitzky in the very beginning.

11. Now? It's time to map out the beats—those phrases, breaths, internal ideas, or momenta that change throughout the monologue—and use them to build a more realized character. Yes, yes. It's time to drop some beats! So, as great actors—THAT'S YOU!—that means reading the monologue again and notating exactly where the beats change. I prefer to use a lightning bolt: ⚡. It reminds me that the energy changes, and that a "spark" of a new action is underway. Also, it's quick to write. You can use whatever symbol you choose to note a beat, just so long as you can SEE IT, and REMEMBER that it represents a BEAT CHANGE.

Example Monologue: Troop 666 with Beat Notations

Hi Mrs. Malcowitzky. Hi. Yes, I know you're sitting shiva... But it's Tuesday, and like you said, Tuesday after 4 but not after 5 would be the best time to stop by. So, here we are. 4:02 on the dot, and I hope we can settle things. (Beat) ⚡Yes, I can see that, Mrs. Malcowitky. So sad. Everyone in black... We are all so very sorry to hear of Mr. Malcowitzky's passing. ⚡He was a wonderful man—a legend really. There's not a kid in the neighborhood that doesn't know how he single-handedly tried to save little Kelly Steven's cat. (Choking up) ⚡In the corner of my mind, I can still see him... Up there, all alone in that big sycamore tree, literally out on a limb for a cat named Spuds. ⚡It was like watching a miracle to see him scamper his, what, 375 pound frame up that tree in like 10 seconds—he was like Spider-Man! And then reach out his fat, fleshy fingers, pull Spuds to him and hold that cat like a newborn babe. ⚡A true hero. And to honor him, you see here? I've immortalized him with a new stripe on my sash. ⚡I embroidered it myself. If you look close, you can even see his smile and his hands around Spuds... before he fell and crushed him, of course. ⚡Yeah. It's not standard GS—that's Girl Scouts—but I got permission to put it on there because of his heroics and, well, because he was such a loyal and faithful customer. ⚡As you know, every year he almost single-handedly sends us—Troop 666—to the national convention. So... ⚡I would hope that, even in death, he would continue to honor his commitments and pay up for all the Do-Si-Dos, Lemonades, Reduced Fat Daisy Go Rounds, and Tagalongs he ordered before his untimely demise. (Beat) ⚡Mrs. Malcowitzky, we know he ordered them... All your guests are eating Thin Mints! (Beat) ⚡Do you want a scene, or do I need to call in more troops? (Beat) ⚡Yes, we take checks.

You'll probably note that some beats are not as "strong" as others, meaning that some only seem to make a slight change, but it is a change nonetheless. Again, as pointed out in Step 9, actively pursuing what you want and choosing an action on either each line or beat brings the piece to life. Now is the time to write those actions in the margin or between the lines of text. Go ahead, do it! It's all for the sake of the work! So? Are you going to chastise, flatter, hurt, threaten, manipulate, bully, impress, provoke, abuse, plead, surprise, help, warn, worry, hassle, prod, enlighten, dare, or play any other wonderful verb on Mr. Malcowitzky to ultimately get what you want? Are you?! Well, you better. Because the woman owes you money! And, also, because after this, you're done. (See the Appendix of Actions for Actors on page 155 to help you get the action juices flowing.)

12. Ok, so you're not *completely* done. There is another question that pertains to just this particular monologue, and an overall question that needs to be answered once you answer the first one. Why do you think you say "Hi" to Mrs. Malcowitzky twice? I'll give you a hint: It has something to do with you being at her door at a time when she'd rather not have you there. The answer to this question will give you added texture as you will know how to respond to Mrs. Malcowitzky's way of being from the very beginning, and this is very important as you need to be responding to how the person you're speaking to is behaving at all times. Although he or she may not be saying anything, it is most important to be responding to his or her way of being. Therefore, ask yourself this last question: "HOW IS THE PERSON I'M SPEAKING TO RESPONDING TO WHAT I'M SAYING AND HOW I'M BEHAVING?" In this monologue example, use your imagination and figure out how Mrs. Malcowitzky is responding and behaving to every

word you say, and let that influence how you behave as well. Sound good? Wonderful!

So there! Phew! You've just broken down a monologue. You've mapped out the beats, written in the actions, and you've answered all the questions: "Who am I?" "To Whom am I speaking?" "When is this taking place?" "Where is this taking place?" "What do I want?" "Why do I want what I want?" "How will I get what I want?" "What happened just before this moment that would have me speak right now?" And finally, "how is the person I'm speaking to responding to what I'm saying and how I'm behaving?" Or, as a short cut, ask: Who, Whom, When, Where, What, Why, How, What and How. Simple! And to make it even easier for you to keep up with your notes, the short cut words are listed after each monologue in this collection. All you need to do is write the answers in, and you'll be off and running. Just remember, you're only limited by your imagination and your willingness to truly BECOME someone. So, have fun. READ! Answer the questions, and take notes. Drop some beats, and play the verbs. And for goodness sakes, read some more! Get to work on becoming. Just take a deep breath, and dive in!

PART ONE: MONOLOGUES FOR YOUNG MEN

TELL ME, MOM

(Danny quietly enters his mother's room. He knows something is not right.)

Danny: Oh... Hi. I'm sorry I woke you. I didn't mean to, but I thought, well... I mean, I hoped that... Uh. Well, Dad said that it was OK if I watched TV, and then he said it would be OK if I ate the Corn Pops, and then he said it would be OK if I ate them all and even from the box. Then he said I could have a dog... Yeah, a dog, a donkey, a small whale, a python, and paint the lawn with yellow spray paint... even dirty words, Mom. He even said yes to that extra large 52-inch plasma from QVC, and then said it was OK to take Grandma down to the skating rink and leave her there if I could sell her to the highest bidder. (Beat) Please Mom, tell me the truth. Just please, don't lie to me. I'm old enough to understand the big stuff. I'm not some kid that's gonna cry... I mean, not like I use to, not like that any more. I can handle it, Mom. Really. I can. Please, just tell me... (Pause) Mom... How sick are you?

Who:

Whom:

When:

Where:

What:

Why:

How:

What:

How:

THE LAST TEN MINUTES

(Jimmy is the coolest kid on the block—the man with the plan—and he knows the importance of helping out a younger kid with his wisdom.)

Jimmy: Put yourself in their shoes... They want you to feel guilty about it. They want you to feel bad. The way I see it, if it weren't for grownups making you feel bad, it would be nothing but chaos and whatchamacallit... Pandemonium. Yeah, pandemonium in the streets. They wouldn't know what to do with themselves. If it wasn't for us kids living our lives and doing what we kids do, grownups would have absolutely nothing to do but go to work and pretend they had someone to yell at for leaving the bike out in the driveway. They'd have to find some other sucker to take the fall for not closing the refrigerator door completely, and that whole "What, were you born in a barn" question would never be uttered again... Who would dry the dishes, rake the lawn, walk the dog, get the paper, set the table, water the plants and do all the little things that make grownups feel so grownup? Listen to me, kid, please... Before completely upsetting the thin balance of humanity we stand on, remember, they were actually kids once. No, really, they were kids once! I didn't believe it at first either, but I've seen pictures and... It's taken me years to get over it, but yup, it's true. All the anger they've held onto for becoming the sad and sick stiffs that they are, is exactly what we need to avoid... Imagine, one day in the near future—I hate to say it, but—there won't be recess. I know, it's a horrible thing, but it <u>will</u> happen. But, it happened to them first... Some saw it coming... Others? They never knew what hit them... They're still waiting for that second bell after lunch... Their last ten minutes in the sun before heading back in for the rest of the day... They never got their last ten minutes and they're taking it out on us. Why? Revenge? Maybe... Negativity? Possible. But I think it's just plain old fear. They're just afraid that we'll actually get our last ten minutes, and in that time find the true meaning of life... something grownups are always saying we'll find out when we grow-up... But then what's the point of growing up if I'm always yelling at a kid? Anyway... (Beat) When you're eleven, like me, you'll understand that it's our responsibility as kids to make them feel good about their "grownupness;" it's our job, our duty to remind them of the ten minutes they lost on the playgrounds across the globe... So, yeah... Draw on the walls with permanent marker... Let flies in, don't put the top on the peanut butter, ruin your dinner with Twinkies... Please, sit as close to the television as possible, and DO NOT wear your slicker in the rain... Keep your chin up, kid. And always remember what I told ya—no matter how many timeouts or groundings you get—without us, they are lost... And without their guilt, we'd never know the value of the last ten minutes. Frightening, yes. But that's the way it is. (Beat) Yeah, even Spider-Man... But I think he got his last ten minutes... The Hulk? I'll have to get back to you on that...

Who:

Whom:

When:

Where:

What:

Why:

How:

What:

How:

THE SWEETEST THING

(Going through puberty is not always easy, and Mickey is doing his best to keep it all together at summer camp.)

Mickey: No, I'm not scared! Shut up... Why should I tell you? All you little grunts want is the nasty details, and I'm not a man to, well, you know... (Beat) Okay, okay. She gave me this locket, and she said... She said, man... She said she loves me. Hey, don't laugh. It's not funny. She actually said that she loves me. She said, I make her smile. Yeah, that's what makes her love me the most. I mean, she said that she saw me from across the room at the barn dance last Wednesday night. I was cool, suave, and all that stuff, if I dare say so myself. I mean, hey, she did say that I was the best dancer... She forgave me for dancing with Gwendolyn Grausburger... She understands that I have an image to keep up. Hey, I am head junior counselor this year. Nothing gets done without my knowledge, and she appreciates that I look out for the little kids, you know? She likes that I do activities that keep most of the fourth grade girls out of the mud and away from the weirdoes in cabin six, 'cause hey, I care about these kids. I care about them because they are my people... Deep down, we are all just like the little freaks, you know? Hey, I know where they're coming from. Anyway... (Pause) I told her I can't see her again..

Hey, it just wouldn't be right. I had to let her go, you know? Hey, if one wants you, they all want you, and this is my last year at camp. I've got to keep the field open, you know? Besides, she thinks I'm this great guy and all, and that I am all these wonderful things... so, like... so... You know, I wasn't always the amazing guy I am now. I wasn't always the great dancer and cool kid that gets the hearts of every sixth grader throbbing, no... I haven't always been great at everything from archery and pottery making, to weaving or other arts and crafts, swimming or water polo... Hey, listen, come on. . . Okay, yeah, I know I was actually a dork once too. . . Yeah, so what if I lost my pants at the talent show four years ago... But I was young, you know? I was just a kid! How the heck did they expect me to make that jump anyway? Peter Pan should fly, but how did they expect me to do that when the harness kept slipping? I thought I'd never live that down, but I turned it all around. I pulled up my pants—and those stupid Red Ranger jockeys—and I made something of myself and something of this camp. And today, well men, I can say that a girl loves me. Laugh all you want, but she loves me for who I am and for who I want to be, and not just because I'm perfect in every possible way. (Beat) What? No, no! That's not true. I am not afraid to—. No way. I'm telling you, it's not like that. I was raised to be a gentleman, and I had to let her down easy... So she wouldn't start crying. You know how women are... They tell you they love you and then you let them down and then they start crying. It's all the same. Every time this happens to me. (Beat) Fine, don't believe me, yeah, just walk away, walk away when I'm trying to school you on the female heart. Walk away when I'm trying to show you how to be strong in the throes of a woman's love. Just walk away when I'm trying to give you the little kernels of wisdom and truth, you jerks! Fine! Just remember, SHE LOVES MOI. Not you nubs. She loves ME and I AM NOT AFRAID—(Looking at the locket.) ...I'm not afraid to kiss her... I'm not.

Who:

Whom:

When:

Where:

What:

Why:

How:

What:

How:

A MAN WITHOUT
A BABYSITTER

(Tyler—who was home without a babysitter for the first time—meets his mother at the door just as the firemen are leaving. He's had a very interesting day.)

Tyler: (To the firemen leaving) Thanks, guys! Thanks! You're the best! Thanks! (Beat) Mom! Mom! No, no... I'm alright. I'm fine, really. The firemen said it's all clear and that we can go in... But...Wait. Wait! Ok. So, I know this doesn't look good, but I want to first say—before you go into the house—I just want to say for the record that I love you more than anything and that I truly appreciate you letting me stay home without a babysitter today. I mean, wow, Mom. Just being who you are—and taking a chance on a kid like me—really says something about you, our relationship, your trust in me and your ability—I hope—to look past my faults and all the little, uhm, stuff, and see the bigger picture. Because! In the bigger pic-ture, I actually learned a lot today! You see, in the "BIGGER PICTURE"—Yes, the bigger picture, Mom—I learned that I am a man with a great mind, with deep sensitivity AND awesome reflexes and Ninja-like agility. For example... when the sofa caught on fire—not my fault, there's a short in the Dust Buster, and you said I had to keep the place clean—but YOU KNOW how much I like to nosh on popcorn and hummus—well, as soon as that thing started blazin', I knew what to do! I grabbed my cup of Yoohoo and dowsed the thing...Tyler ONE. Fire ZERO! But being that the Dust Buster was still plugged in, well, it sparked again and some landed on Fluffy. She's Ok! (Beat) Except for a bit of a bald spot... But that was not my fault either because if she would have just stopped, dropped and rolled like I kept telling her, and hadn't climbed the curtains, then I could have put her out faster. But cats? They're like from a different planet... Well... Anyway, I put her out—Yoohoo-style—only to notice that your curtains were a bit singed and starting to smoke, and being that I was out of Yoohoo, I did the next best thing. I ripped off my shirt, soaked it in the sink, and beat your curtains till they stopped burning. (Beat) It wasn't until then that I noticed the broken china. Apparently, Fluffy doesn't like Yoohoo. She flipped out, started running all over the place, then jumped on the mantle and knocked down all of Grandma's china, which is not my fault because I know Dad said you should have secured it to the wall and not just on the little china tripod-thingies because—as he's said before—you really should secure that china because at the end of the world there will probably be an earthquake or typhoon or something, and the china probably won't make it. Well, Fluffy was that typhoon, and the typhoon won. Typhoon TEN. Tyler TWO. So... I was just grateful that the house wasn't on fire, but I felt so bad for the cat, you know? I really wanted to make it up to her, but being that I don't speak her cat language, she ran out of the pet door in the kitchen and up the oak tree in the neighbor's yard, so I just did what came natural, ran after her and started climbing the tree to get her. I know how much you love that cat, Mom, and I wasn't about to just leave her up there. So! I was up there in like five secs! Tyler THREE. Oak tree, like NOTHIN'! But the darn cat wouldn't come to me—not like I blamed her. But I didn't give up, and just kept climbing and climbing. And wow. That's a pretty old oak tree. Pretty tall... (Beat) Hey. Did you know that we have new neighbors?! I didn't know that! 'Cause I was like way up there and then I heard this girl's voice from below, you know? She was like, "Hey! What are you doing in our tree?" And I was like, "Hey! Like, I'm trying to save my mother's cat!" And then she was like, "Ok..." (Beat) "But why aren't you wearing any pants?" Man, in all the commotion, I forgot that I hadn't put any pants on. So while I was climbing down, I was like, Embarrassed ONE MILLION. Tyler like zip! (Aside) Wait. Why do I keep saying "Like"? Anyway... I locked myself out, which is not my fault because the back door has that automatic lock and I didn't have time to get my key AND chase after Fluff, you know? I mean, grabbing my key wasn't on my radar... So! I was without keys or pants, and I'm sure it would have made the average dude really antsy, but Mom, you'd be so proud of me. I sucked up my pride, made friends with Megan—the new girl next door—and she let me borrow a pair of her dad's pants. We were just hanging out in her backyard waiting for Fluffy to come down or you to come home...and in that time I really learned a lot about Megan, her love of the dance, and her fear of raccoons, popsicles and small children with green eyes that wear wide-brimmed hats... Something about the Children of the Corn movies... Anyway... I think we are on our way to making this one summer to remember, especially since—and this is important because this part kinda IS my fault... I was over at Meg's—that's what I call her now, Meg—yeah, I was over there for like five hours, maybe more, and that whole time I had forgotten that I, well, uhm, well, I still hadn't unplugged the Dust Buster... (Beat) So, now, before you go inside, I just want to say that I take full responsibility for what you're about to, you know, see... and smell... But if you think about it, in the bigger picture, all if this happened for a good reason, you know? I learned that I have great Yoohoo and tree climbing skills, that I can think quick on my feet, that cats are very sensitive and "different" animals, that girls are kinda cool, and that I'm kinda cool because I learned all that on my own. Plus! Meg and I have a date this Friday!!! Tyler A BILLION. Other dudes, ziltch! And that's all thanks to you because you let me stay home without a babysitter. Thanks, Mom. Well, anyway... I'll let you take a peak inside... You just go ahead... As for me, I'll just try that oak tree one more time. Fluff, well, she's still up there and I forgot to tell the firemen to go up and get her... But that was not my fault, I mean, with the back of the house on fire, who has time to say, "Like, dude, my mother's cat is ALSO in the neighbor's tree?" Ha! You know? Like, who?

Who:

Whom:

When:

Where:

What:

Why:

How:

What:

How:

HIDEAWAY PINES

(Milo finally tells his Grandfather what's really going on.)

Milo: Uh, Grandpa. A wise man once told me, never forget where you come from, son. And never forget the good ones who come along with you. You can rely on them because they'll be there with you in the end. I assumed you were talking about you and me, so as a "good" one, I can't let you leave the room like that. Not that I'm some sort of fashion expert, but I don't think green and white golf shorts were ever meant to be worn with a yellow polo shirt, an orange blazer, or lavender suspenders, with a matching pocket square, and bow tie. Oh, right. AND, a tweed, flat cap. Can't forget the flat cap. Nothing says I'm 87-years-old and looking for action like a tweed, flat cap. Nice. (Beat) Look, I get that you're trying to make a name for yourself here at Hideaway Pines now that, well, now that Grandma is... Well, now that Grandma has been moved across the hall... And I know that you're still hip—or, as mom would say, "still using your original hip"—but I don't think a man of your distinguished stuff and abilities should ever be caught alive or dead wearing black socks with sandals. Really. No. Really, Grandpa, it's like looking at all of Florida and knowing life is going to end badly... One black sock and sandal at a time. Please. Just take them off. I can dig the flat cap—I can—and your take on colorblind dressing, but the black socks and sandals make me want to take all of *your* medications...at the same time. So... Yeah. Thanks. So... Now that I have your undivided attention—and since it's going to take you at least another half an hour to reach down there and take off those socks—JUST JOSHIN!—I think it's time we talk about the elephant in the room, or should I say, the Grandma NOT in the room. (Deep sigh) I know everyone else has been trying to spare your feelings and tiptoe around the subject, but you and I have always, you know... It's always been you and me against the world, and we've always stuck up for each other... Like, when I accidentally hit that baseball through the upstairs window, you told mom that you did it. When you accidentally sliced that golf ball through the back sliding glass, and it hit Aunt Helen so hard that her dentures flew out, I told Grandma that I did it. And when I couldn't get my volcano to erupt with more umph, you suggested that I mix the red food dye with baking soda, vinegar AND gasoline for more, well, umph. Yeah, so... We lit it. Ok. But, I never squealed to mom or Grandma about how that patch of grass in the back suddenly got charred, and you never punked out and cried about how your toupee suddenly looked crispy around the edges. I mean, we've been there for each other. For forever. (Beat) So, it took a little while, but sure, I was cool with you and Grandma moving out, and moving here to Hideaway Pines. Which is the dumbest name for this place because you can see it right off the highway, and there isn't a pine tree in a thousand miles, but hey, you two wanted to be in an "assisted living"-retirement-condo-sexy-old-folky-hangy-outy-place. That's cool. Alright. Ok. Do what you have to do. It's all good. It's what you both wanted. But then you got here and... Being around all these other people, you just...The new clothes, the new hat... And now with Grandma gone... Well, I mean, she's not really GONE. She's just across the hall. (Beat) Ok, listen. I know I shouldn't tell you this because she told me that she'd choke me until my eyes popped out of my head, write me out of her will and then burn this place to the ground, but, listen... Grandma is in no way suffering from dementia. Not even close, Grandpa. The only reason she's over there, across the hall, *PRETENDING* that she can't remember you, your life together, and all that you've been through over the last 67 years is because you've changed! You've changed, man! Hanging out every morning with the shuffleboard dudes that drink White Russians at the pool and spout dirty limericks at the visiting nurses. Up, playing strip canasta on Monday nights with those giggly widows from the third floor, and strip mahjong with the giggly widows from the fifth floor on Tuesdays. Miniature trains with your buddies on Wednesday and Thursday afternoons, and Dance Party USA with the retired marines on Fridays... You've got yoga, jiu jitsu, defensive driving in the 21st Century, Urban Archeology classes, Ageless Mind and Body Connection Intensives, Parallel Parking a Golf Cart for Dummies tutorials, and that online course to get your certificate in Graphic Design. And in all of it—ALL OF IT—you totally left Grandma out. You just went off, made plans, or signed yourself up without her. Dude. She told me that just last week you did an impromptu belly dance in the rec room during the screening of her favorite movies! Coccoon AND Coccoon The Return! Grandpa! Even I know not to do that! That's like the holy grail of holy movie grails for old people! (Beat) So, man, whatever this is about—whatever all this pimp-daddy-stylin'—is all about, it's not working, man. (Beat) Look, you and Grandma have always been there for me and mom. Always. And, you and me? You and me are forever. I know that—'cause you've been my best bud, grandfather, cool dude and all, for my whole life—always there...And I get that you need to have your time to be, you know, YOU. But even I know that the coolest, hottest, most amazing, sweetest, dopest, most rad chick on the "assisted living"-retirement-condo-sexy-old-folky-hangy-outty-block is Grandma, and although she's pretending to have forgotten you, you really did forget her. That ain't cool, Grandpa. It ain't cool. (Beat) You know, a wise man once told me, never forget where you come from, son. And never forget the good ones who come along with you. You can rely on them because they'll be there with you in the end. And you know what Grandpa, you were right.

Who:

Whom:

When:

Where:

What:

Why:

How:

What:

How:

THE PLAN

(Justin Allan Lemar Tenant—the most forthright kid on the planet—is going on his first date. There is not a trace of sarcasm or cynicism in his body, and if he could plan out how the world should run, he'd do it! Note: Justin indicates with his fingers whenever there are quotation marks. Also, Justin can be from almost anywhere—from The Bronx, to Tennessee, to Southern California—so play around with different regional accents.)

Justin: Hello Mr. Schmechkenbaum. I'm Justin Allan Lemar Tenant, but everyone just calls me Justin Allan Lemar. I'm here to pick up Ellie... Thanks for letting me come by a little early, you know, so we can get acquainted, lay down some guidelines—a plan, if you will. (Aside) Is it ok if I leave my Schwinn out front? Ok. Great. So! Well, first I'd like to say that the plan for tonight is a brief bite at McDonald's or Wendy's—depending on Ellie's preference of French fries and/or Frosty—followed by a short but brisk walk around the parking lot to aid in digestion before heading to the 3:30 screening of the latest Harry Potter film. I assume we will chat about the film afterward—taking a slightly longer route back here to give us time to compare all the plot points, nuances of the main characters, direction, special effects, and how closely the production has stuck to the book. If the date proceeds without a "hitch," I then plan to date Ellie for the remainder of 8th Grade and throughout our high school careers... Weekend dates, Homecoming, Proms, etc., etc., and in this time become closer, of course, but will maintain a "youthful," if not "innocent," connection of respect and friendship for one another. Anyway, then will come college. I know Ellie likes frogs, so I assume she will be applying to a university that will support this passion and study—say, Columbia University—where she will earn her Bachelors of Science in Botany or Chemical Engineering. Frog slime has many useful chemical compounds, you know. Yes, she will work towards her goals at Columbia while I complete my double major in Astrophysics and Religion at Yale. We will do a lot of emailing and Skyping, of course, but much more when she goes off to complete her graduate degree and research somewhere in the Amazon. As for me, I will be at Princeton completing my doctoral thesis on black holes and their gravitational pull on the Ten Commandments. Then, we'll get married, of course, get a nice place near NYU—naturally we'll be professors—and from there have 2.5 kids. I'm not sure about the ".5," but I assume that's a dog... or a frog, depending on what Ellie brings back from the Amazon. (Looks at his watch) Well, look at the time. I'm sure Ellie will be down in a moment, so... I'd like to gather my thoughts before she descends from upstairs. I truly appreciate your time and consideration, Mr. Schmechkenbaum, and really look forward to us discussing retirement... As for Ellie and me, I expect to discuss this full plan—our "objectives of this relationship"—over a nice cold bottle of water on the way home. No worries, sir. I'll have Ellie back no later than, 7:30. Should you have any questions or concerns, here's my card. Thank you, sir. Thank you.

Who:

Whom:

When:

Where:

What:

Why:

How:

What:

How:

THE SECOND DATE

(Robbie puts his foot down when his grandmother goes on a date.)

Robbie: I think it's time I make it clear where I stand on all of this, Mom... Dad... And I think you should know before we get in too deep. (Takes a puff from his inhaler). Listen, I can deal with the dudes in the hallways...Gabe, Mac, Jesse and all those guys. I can put up with Margie Rothesberger and her crew of freckled-faced hens cackling when I walk by. I can even ignore Avi Mendelstein making kissy faces and smashing his lips up against his wriggling hand while I'm practicing my haftorah—Yeah, he looks like he's sucking face with a squid—but I can handle that, 'cause it's Hebrew school and sometimes you just gotta do what you just gotta do. You ask why? (Takes a quick puff.) 'Cause in just two short weeks I'm going to be called to the bema and become a man. I KNOW—beyond a shadow of a doubt!—that I can become that man because I believe in myself, in my faith and in my family. But this?! Nooo... This is BEYOND belief, beyond faith and beyond anything from which I could ever—EVER!—recover. I'm serious, people! Extra therapy WON'T fix this! This will forever be burned into my psyche... My VERY SOUL! I mean, did you even see what she was wearing when she left? Come on, people! You let her go out of here wearing a dress that was up to here, and a top that showed the tops of her—You know! Her parts! (Beat) Geez Louise, people! Her...parts! (Beat) Do you even know what's happening here? Do you even have a clue?! She's going on her second date! Grandma is on HER SECOND DATE!! This isn't something to get excited about! NO! The second date is the, well, the "YOU KNOW" date... Don't you people watch any shows on Fox? The second date is THE DATE THAT STUFF HAPPENS ON! AND YOU JUST LET HER GO OUT THERE LIKE A LAMB TO THE SLAUGHTER! Don't you care? Don't you have any sense of decency... Any sense of family pride??? She left with her parts showing, and you think it's just dandy! (Takes a puff from his inhaler.) It's bad enough that I have to deal with the stupidity at school with all the kids making fun of me over this... I mean, I still try to keep my sense of loyalty even though my grandma is dating our Rabbi! I don't think it's Kosher, but what do I know? Huh? And what do you care?! You don't have to stand next to this guy in two weeks knowing he went on TWO DATES WITH MY BUBBIE WHEN HER-HER-HER BUBBIES WERE SHOWING! It's supposed to be hava nagila, not HAVA-MY-GRANDMA! (Takes a long puff on his inhaler.) But I know what to do... Oh, yes. I know what to do to make you fix this. 'Cause you are going to fix this, people! You're either going to break them up, or I am going to my bar mitvah WITHOUT my inhaler. And you KNOW what that means... Oh, yes you do! That means that only one of two things can happen should you refuse to keep them apart: 1.) I die... And you'll have wasted all this money on a chocolate fountain, a hip-hop dance team and chicken fingers shaped like sombreros, or 2.) I die, you'll have wasted all this money, and will have to restore this family's integrity because Grandma will have gone on her THIRD DATE with Rabbi Nussbaum! And that, my friends, is a move YOU DO NOT want to make. Second dates are risky, but the third?! There's no telling what parts she'll be showing by then! (Takes a quick inhale, holds it. Then:) No telling! (Beat) So what's it gonna be, folks? What's it gonna be? My life... or Bubbie's...parts? (Beat) Parts... or life? (Beat) It's either THIS (holds up his inhaler)... or all of THIS (gestures to his chest). I think it's pretty crystal clear... But this is your decision. It's on you, people. It's all on you... (Beat) So, please, do the right thing... (As if giving them the choice again, he takes a quick inhale, nods "yes", then gestures to his chest, shakes his head "no"... He walks away...)

Who:

Whom:

When:

Where:

What:

Why:

How:

What:

How:

THE FORCE

(Josh is dressed in all black, is wearing a Darth Vader mask, and is carrying a backpack.)

Josh: (He breathes heavily, clears his throat, then lifts the mask.) Hi, Julia! Oh, sorry I scared you. Again... Oh, gosh. I hope you understand that I'm not doing this on purpose. It's just that it's Tuesday, and as you know, I prefer to go with Darth Vader on Tuesdays. Obi-wan on Mondays, Vader on Tuesdays, Yoda on Wednesdays, Luke on Thursdays, and Leia on Fridays... And that's only if my mom can get those fresh challah cinnamon rolls from Whole Foods. (He mimes holding the bread up to his head for Leia's hair). If she can't get the challah, then I try to mix it up and go with Boba Fett, Lando Calrissian, or C3PO. You know, with my narrow hips and longish legs, C3PO really suits me. I mean, look at these legs? It's a curse, really. But I digress... (Pause) You know, I really appreciate that you never judge me for my love of the original Star Wars Trilogy. Really. I mean, you offered to have me sit with you on the bus on the first day of Pre-K and even helped me sit down when my R2-D2 suit got me stuck in the aisle... Wow... All these years, and you're like the only person that never says anything. In fact, you're the only one—other than my mom and dad— that doesn't freak out about it. Not that I really care what other people say... I'm my own man. But, well... it's much appreciated, and, well... (He clears his throat.) So... did you get my note? I know. It's so old school. A "note"... I'm sure a text would have been just as appropriate, but I believe that these things require more of a "personal touch". You know, it required boldness... Sorta like when Luke rescues Leia on the Death Star.... (He smiles and laughs to himself. Then clears his throat.) Did you notice that it was scented? The note? I scented it. Axe For Men... Not my personal favorite, but Walmart was running a promotional. Two Star Wars costumes and you got anything else half off. I went with the Axe for Men... I felt it would be the most appropriate scent that, say, a hero in space would use to attract the opposite sex. For me it was a bit risky, but again, bold. Sort of like when Leia takes the opportunity to strangle Jabba the Hut while wearing the equivalent to a cut out breastplate, dental floss, and strategically placed curtains and eyeliner in Return of the Jedi. (Clears his throat). Anyway... did you notice the boxes? You know, the boxes in the note? (Pause) Oh, you've misplaced the note? Hmmm... (Beat) Well, no worries! I have several copies here on hand. (He pulls out two huge handfuls of folded notes from his backpack.) And they are all scented... (He drops several.) Oops... (He unfolds a note and holds it up. There are several boxes with choices next to them to choose from. 1. You really like me. 2. You kinda like me. 3. You like me, but not in that way. 4. You are not sure of any kind of liking of me. And 5. You do not like me.) Okay, so as you can see here, I've created a simple "tool", if you will, that will help you and I come to an understanding. Clear, simple, and concise. (He clears his throat, then he reads the note.) I'll just read it to you... (Reading) Dear Julia, here is a simple tool, if you will, that will help you and I come to an understanding. It is clear, simple, and concise. Just check the appropriate box and/or boxes that apply. 1.) You really like me. 2.) You kinda like me. 3.) You like me, but not in that way. 4.) You are not sure of any kind of liking of me. And 5.) You do not like me. Also, you should know that I have loved you since the moment I met you. I have loved you with a deeper love than I love my dog, all my Star Wars action figures, all my Star Wars space vehicle collections, and all my Star Wars costumes—well, almost all of them. I have loved you with a devotion that will span the test of time and the vastness of space...past the planets of my heart and beyond the beyond, because to me, you *are* The Force... Thank you very much. Signed, Yours truly, Josh. PS. If you lose this note, please don't worry, I have copies. (Beat) Ok... So... Well, you just think about it— the choices, that is—and get back to me at your earliest convenience. I know you're very busy, so I promise to be patient. Cool? Cool... (He smiles and turns to walk away, but then turns to her again.) I'll be as patient as Han Solo was while waiting for that first kiss from Leia on the planet of Endor in the Empire Strikes Back... You know, with all the Ewoks and stuff... Right. (He smiles.)

Who:

Whom:

When:

Where:

What:

Why:

How:

What:

How:

MY HERO

(Eric has come to terms with what he must do to truly be himself. Note: This monologue stands on its own, but it can be paired with "The Force" in a reading. Therefore, it is suggested that one should read "The Force" as well.)

Eric: (He sighs, then-) I found a bunch of these notes on the floor at school today... At first, I was totally laughing my butt off, but... I want you to hear this, OK? No, really. You gotta hear this. (Reading) Dear Julia, here is a simple tool, if you will, that will help you and I come to an understanding. It is clear, simple, and concise. Just check the appropriate box and/or boxes that apply. 1.) You really like me. 2.) You kinda like me. 3.) You like me, but not in that way. 4.) You are not sure of any kind of liking of me. And 5.) You do not like me. (Beat) Also, you should know that I have loved you since the moment I met you. I have loved you with a deeper love than I love my dog, all my Star Wars action figures, all my Star Wars space vehicle collections, and all my Star Wars costumes—well, almost all of them. I have loved you with a devotion that will span the test of time and the vastness of space... past the planets of my heart and beyond the beyond, because to me, you *are* The Force... Thank you very much. Yours truly, Josh. PS. If you lose this note, please don't worry, I have copies. (Beat) Yeah. It's from that

Josh Brainard dude. You know, the kid everyone messes with 'cause he's like addicted to Star Wars. No, it's not like an addiction, it's like HE IS Star Wars. He wrote this to Julia Formidgen. Like, THE hottest girl in our class. Maybe the whole school... And I'll tell ya, I was gonna show it to all the guys because I knew they'd totally give him crap for it, you know? Totally. And everyone would say how stupid he was for even trying...I mean, Julia Formidgen! Come on! (Beat) But then something happened to me, something powerful that just stopped me in my tracks...I just... I just...(Beat) You know, I've been going over and over in my mind how I was gonna say this to you since between seventh and eighth period today. I mean, you've been my hero for, like, my whole life. I was the Robin to your Batman, the Watson to your Sherlock Holmes... The Bubba to your Forrest Gump. You get the picture? Everything you did and everything you told me to do, I took on because you said so. Like when I gave up chess because you said it was for kids that think too much... And when I gave up water polo because you said it was just one step away from synchronized swimming. I gave up theatre classes because you said it was for babies that can't deal with reality. That, and tether ball, horseback riding, tennis—because it was for snobs—fishing, because it was for old people, and bowling because it was never a real sport. You said, "Real dudes play football. Real dudes get hit and get hit hard because that's cool. Wear the right clothes, sport the right gear, and get with the hottest girl. Stay away from the weird kids... The ones that ride unicycles, the ones that wear capes, ones that ride unicycles AND wear capes, ones that wear costumes, and ones that don't have their own Facebook page. Then you'll be cool, and that is the only way to make it in school. Anything but that is worthless." And because you're my brother, I believed you. And for years, I've been trying to be "that cool". Didn't get me on the football team though... And although I got mom to get me "the right clothes" and "the right gear", it still didn't get me the hottest girl. If anything, it makes me look like 95% of the other kids I know, and most of them, frankly, aren't that cool either. 'Cause they don't take any risks, or make any real difference because...because any real difference would mean letting people see how different we really are... (Beat) I've never done that. But Josh Brainard has... Josh Brainard took a chance, showed the world how truly different he really is, and totally made a difference. At least in my mind, because today—TODAY—the whole school saw Julia Formidgen—THE HOTTEST GIRL IN SCHOOL!—kiss Josh Brainard on the mouth like no one's business. Yes, TODAY, the girl every dude is totally into, made out with Darth Vader at the lockers between seventh and eighth period. And it totally messed with my head! (Pause) I saw Darth Vader in a lip lock with Julia Formidgen, and neither one of them looked like they cared what ANYONE thought... Stopped me in my tracks. Stopped me in my tracks because I started thinking, what would I do if I just went for it, you know? What would happen if I went for something that really made me happy and stopped caring what everyone—even my big brother, my hero—thinks about it? Who would I be in the face of that? ...And in that moment, Josh Brainard became my new hero. Darth Vader and all... (Beat) I just thought you should know that. (Pause) I'm gonna go find a frame for this note... and then dust off my chess set... You're welcome to come join me... I mean, if you're ready to take a chance, I think Josh Brainard could be your hero too... (Beat) Wow... Really? Oh, yeah, sure... You can even have your own copy. (He pulls out two handfuls of Josh's notes from his back pocket.) I have tons. (Sniffs them.) And I think they're all scented...

Who:

Whom:

When:

Where:

What:

Why:

How:

What:

How:

LEAVIN'

(After his father's death, James has watched his mother sink farther and farther into a dangerous relationship with a man that hits her.)

James: Ten short-stemmed yellow roses and a card... Do you really think it matters? Do you think it makes a difference? Really? Does this make it all better for you? 'Cause from where I'm standing, it just don't add up... You got needs. We got needs. I got needs, too. Needs that have needs, and I ain't just a kid. (Beat) I got potential. Yeah, potential. And if it was up to me, I'd take Jamie and that damn car, and get the hell out of here. 'Cause waiting around for you to take my father's keys outta that old box and drive us off into the sunset is just as real as that little farm upstate with the white picket fence and the duck pond... Don't tell me that it's real. I know the truth. And the truth hurts, don't it? Like thorns on ten short-stemmed yellow roses. It hurts when you hold 'em wrong. But I know how to hold 'em... Set 'em in a place in my mind... a place where it's quiet at night... a place where the hum of fluorescents don't chase you from room-to-room and call out your name in red and blue flashes... where your sister doesn't cry herself to sleep, pouring out disappointment and hiding under the covers. She ain't afraid of the Boogie Man—even he's too scared to show his face around here. And there's a place where... where your own mother can sit after a long day's work and put her feet up, instead of getting down on her knees every night, trying to play perfect...trying to scrub the stench of her own dead dreams out of the kitchen floor. The same floor that her new boyfriend just loves to send her sailing across... (Beat) But I got potential. I got potential and a need that's stronger than this place, or some guy that sends you cheap roses and throws low punches. He is not the stars in the night sky, he is not all the heavens above. You are not the moon, and he is not the sun. I am. I am the son, your son! And my life does not revolve around you and your need to be "perfect" for a ten short stemmed, yellow rose jerk. (Beat) And if you're not careful... If you're not careful, Mama, my need... My need, well, it's gonna mean leavin' you... And leavin' soon. (Beat) Humph, it's not even a Hallmark card.

Who:

Whom:

When:

Where:

What:

Why:

How:

What:

How:

FAT LIP

(Lonny will be 18-years-old in fifteen minutes, and tonight, he's taking his future in his own hands and putting his step-father in his place.)

Lonny: I ain't leavin'. Fine, whatever makes you happy. You wanna hit me? Hit me. You wanna see me fall to the floor? Fine. You wanna see me get up and take it again? You know you wanna see me take it again...You been doin' that for forever, so I don't think this one's gonna be any different... 'Cept this time, I ain't cryin'. This time is the last time you see me cry. Last time you see me weak, last time you see me crawl away. Last time—you're allowed—to hit me. I'll give you that. Hell, we'll call it my birthday present... for old times sake, so come on. Get it over with. Bust my nose, bruise my face... I still ain't leavin'. Call me names and say that I ain't no good, just like my father. Just like him, sad and pathetic with nothing to give and only a beating to take... Fine. I still ain't leavin'. I ain't leavin' my brothers and sisters behind with you. Hey, you can even pull out your weapon of choice, but this is my time. This is it. Get it? This is it, so bring it. Do it. Do it now before you change your mind and start thinkin' you may be makin' a mistake; before you search too damn deep into your so-called soul and find you been wrong. (Beat) You ain't got second thoughts now, do you? No. Not you. Not even when I begged you to stop did you ever listen... Not when my arm was broke, my hair pulled out, and when you, oops, "accidentally" busted all my birthday gifts and damn near all my teeth that one year. No, you never stopped 'cause I was just that bad. I deserved it. "A kid gotta learn yearly 'cause youth is wasted on the young." Well, I'll be eighteen in fifteen minutes and then we'll see. Yeah, we'll see. 'Cause in a little while... It all belongs to me. My life. Mine. Don't say I didn't warn you. Don't say I didn't tell you first... I'm giving you that "respect," at least to warn you. Givin' you that "step-dad respect," right? That "step-dad, I'm the better man in town, so do as I say or get beat down, step-dad respect," right? I'm givin' it to you, man. Givin' it up for you. But just remember, you gotta go to sleep sometime. You gotta close your eyes sometime, and when you do, when you close ya lids remember I never asked for nothin', never got nothin' but this (shows bruises), and this, and this from you. Not a father... But since you ain't got that in you, since you ain't got but two fists, I'll give you your last due. Your last due... My last fat lip... My last. 'Cause I ain't leavin'... But I think we know who is... One way or another... (Beat) You ready? Alright... Let's do this.

Who:

Whom:

When:

Where:

What:

Why:

How:

What:

How:

THE BREAK LINE

(Brian and Sam were actually invited to the "coolest" graduation party of the year, but something goes wrong and Brian wants revenge. Only problem is, Sam may not have followed instructions.)

Brian: This has got to be the best idea I have ever had. Ok, ok. So you made sure that nobody saw you, right? Right? Sam? Sam! Ok, you're freaking me out, man. I've been waiting half a good Saturday to get this guy, and this is killer! (He laughs.) I cannot wait to see his dumb-ass face when his engine light comes on half way down the block and that puppy starts clunking and sputtering. Smoke shooting out the tail! I hate to have to put out so much pollutant, but he asked for it. He asked for it! He thinks he can come up in my neighborhood, and be around my friends, and come up in Alaina's house like he owns the place and think he can get away with that?! Nobody calls me a tree hugging freak and gets away with it. Nobody. Especially some flat-headed puke that doesn't even know how to spell hybrid. Ugh. Look at that. No consideration for the environment, so I have no consideration for his gas guzzling, carbon emitting, overpriced, early-21st century status, yet pathetically out of synch yuppy- mobile. It's time for a little payback. No. It's time for some big payback. (He smiles.) Ok, you're right. We should go back in before anybody misses us. (Pause) So, you made sure to cut the left one, right? Sam? I just asked you a question. Sam! What do you mean what? I just asked you a question. I asked you a simple question, Sam. You made sure to only cut the left one. (Beat) What? You what? It was so simple... What did I tell you, Sam? No... I said to cut the left one... (Beat, slow fear sets in.) You idiot! Oh my god! Which part of your brain are you using?! Come on!! What the hell! I've seen you working on your dad's car all the time! I thought you knew! I mean, I saw it on a Spike TV show about cars. It was always on the left! All you had to do was cut the left one and when he drives away then the red light would come on. It's the oil line, no big deal. If you cut the other one then- You cut the brakes??! You cut the brake line, Sam! YOU CUT THE BRAKES! Sam! Oh my god! Sam, man! You gotta fix it. You gotta go fix it. What do you mean me? Me? I didn't cut the brakes, Sam! I didn't- No, no way... I told you to cut the left one. I told you to cut the oil line. The OIL line!! What the hell, Sam! I wanna scare the dude not kill'em! Oh god! He's gonna die. If he gets in that car and drives off, he'll have no brakes, Sam. He'll have no brakes and then we're going down for murder! You're only fourteen, but I'm eighteen in six days, man! That's adult, Sam! We have to figure out how to keep him from getting in his car. We have to distract him. Maybe you could... No, that's stupid, maybe if... No, that would cause a fire... Crap! Think of something, Sam! Crap!!! I hate him even more now that I know he's going to die and send me to prison! Then again, maybe he deserves to die. He is an asshole. Oh my god, what am I saying? Sam! I've got a full ride to Montpelier. I'm the first in my family to go to college, Sam. I had a full ride, man! I was going to be a botanist! I was gonna study plants and save the planet, but now I've just killed a dude. No, no. I can't go to prison! I'm still- I'm still a virgin, man. Do you know what they do to virgins in prison?! Do you have any idea what they do to white, suburban virgins in prison, Sam?! What the hell did you do?! What the hell did you do to me, Sam—(Beat) Why are you laughing? This crap's not funny, Sam. Stop laughing! You cut the dude's brake line, and—Wait. You... You... You... didn't...cut...his...brake line did you? (Long pause) You didn't cut anything, did you?

Who:

Whom:

When:

Where:

What:

Why:

How:

What:

How:

MY GIRL MINI

(While at a blowout birthday party, Schylar's girlfriend, Mini, has locked herself in the bathroom after telling him some devastating news that could impede on their future together. Throughout the monologue he tries to be quiet, but forceful.)

Schylar: Open the f-ing door, Mini! Got-dang! Open the door, M! You can't just walk up and tell me that, then run away like some stupid kid and expect that I would just stand there... What did you expect me to do? Huh? What did you expect me to do? M! M! I know you can hear me! I know you can... Can you? Can you hear me? We can get through it. And yes, it's a "we" thing. It's a "we" thing, M. From day one, you told me that if we were gonna be together—if we were gonna make a go of it— that no matter what happened, we were gonna be a WE, remember? I'm keeping my end of the bargain, M. I'm keeping my word. You're my girl, and whatever happens, then... Then bring it. Bring it! I'm here, and I'm not letting something, something like this—No! I'm not letting something like this get in the way of us being together. (Beat) I know you're scared. I'm scared too, M. I'm scared you don't believe me. I'm scared that you're in there thinking that I'm gonna run out on you when you start those treatments... I'm scared you won't want to see me when that stuff starts working on your insides and you won't let me hold your hair when you have to puke your brains out. Or let me see you when your hair is gone... I'm scared that you're in there thinking that I won't see the most beautiful girl still living in you—the girl that will let me hold her hand when she needs it, kiss her head before it hits the pillow, or let me see her cry when nobody else is around. But most of all, I'm scared that you'll push me out 'cause of some word—a word called leukemia that will end up being like this door, and I'll be stuck on the outside trying to get in and hold you. Do you hear what I'm saying to you, woman? Do you? Crap! Mini! Open the door! Open the door, Mini, and let me in... You don't have to do this on your own... Baby, please... I... I love you, M. I love you, Mini. And that is bigger than that disease, stronger than this f-ing door, and more powerful than any chemo or radiation... or your stubborn self. So get that! Get it, because I'm not going! Except maybe to get you a piece of cake. I expect the door to be unlocked by the time I get back, OK, M? OK?! M?! (He listens, she says, OK. He smiles.) OK. (Beat) And if you tell my boys I said any of that, well... (Pause) Well, you can just tell'em whatever you want. I'll make sure to get you extra icing. I know how you like it...

Who:

Whom:

When:

Where:

What:

Why:

How:

What:

How:

PART TWO: MONOLOGUES FOR YOUNG MEN AND YOUNG WOMEN

INVESTED

(Our hero is on the side of the road in the hot sun, and things are not looking good.)

If I have to walk one more mile, I swear I'm gonna explode. That's it, that's it, that is it! No more paper route—No more! No more dogs, no more biking uphill—both ways—and no more rabid, Ninja kindergarteners jumping out of the hedges... What is up with that? That crap's not funny. I quit... I mean, what does a kid have to do to get any respect in this town? (Beat) You know, I don't have to be "considerate" of my customers... I'm the only one that keeps the Evening Gazette out of the gutters, the mud puddles, the flowerbeds... How many rose bushes can one neighborhood have? Tell me, when one neighbor puts in roses, does everyone have to follow? Did I miss the memo? Why did Mrs. Greyson's <u>ONE</u> rose bush constitute a three mile rose garden extravaganza? This is not a competition people! It's all in your heads. And now in my sinuses! I'm allergic to roses! But what do you all care? Ha! But you still expect me to be pleasant when I come to your boiling-cabbage-smelling houses—cabbage wrapped in old bologna more like it. Has anyone heard of Lysol? A scented Plug-In, maybe? For heaven's sake, even I keep my room smelling summertime fresh in case someone pops by. But not you people. No, it's always, "Boil that cabbage and get the bologna ready, I can see the paper kid coming... Coming to beg." Yeah, beg because you cheapskates NEVER pay on time. There's always an excuse, "I'll have it next week. Just come by next week." Or, "My husband takes care of that, but he's not home now... I'm sure he'll take care of it soon." And my favorite: "Do you take credit cards?" What? Do I look like I can carry a credit card swipe AND thirty-five pounds of newspapers? It ain't part of my job description... But hey, maybe I'll suggest it to the boss that he uplink my body so you crooks can slide your stinking Diner's Club Card through my butt cheeks. IT'S A LOUSY SIX BUCKS PEOPLE! (Breaking down) And now... Now when I could use some help... Now, when my bike blows BOTH tires, no one will help me... Not one, not one of you ungrateful slugs. You drive past and you... you wave? Why are you waving?! Come on! Help a kid out! Pull over, pick me up and help me! (Beat) But that's not who you are... I'm the considerate one... I'm the good kid that cares about you people... I'm part of the information super highway too, man, and I'm out here— out here!—walking the streets alone delivering precious cargo to a bunch... to a bunch of creeps that don't even care that I've invested my blood, sweat, and tears into a business that I was good at... no, great at... a business that—if you would have shown just a little gratitude, a little respect—could have lasted more than four days. But no... It was just too much to ask. Just too darn much, so I quit. I quit. I QUIT!

Who:

Whom:

When:

Where:

What:

Why:

How:

What:

How:

SOFT

(Mark/Maria explains to the hospital social worker why he/she doesn't like hard things.)

Mark/Maria: I don't understand. How could it be bad to like soft things? I like soft things. Soft is good. Not hard things. Hard things are bad. They are bad because they are not, you know, soft. And that's what makes soft things so good. (Beat) You don't get it, do you? Okay, so I'll give you an example... Soft things are huggable and you can squeeze them without breaking them. Hard things can break and that's not good 'cause if you break somethin', you get in trouble and you get a spanking and you have to go to the closet without supper and you can't come out for a long time and you have to stay there in the dark and think about why you're so dumb and why you were born in the first place to such a perfect Mommy that has done nothing but sacrifice her own dreams to raise your stupid self... (Beat) So... If things were soft, like my teddy is, well then they wouldn't break. Well, unless you drop something by accident—something hard like a television—and then your Mommy rips your teddy's arms off and beats you with them... That's the only way soft things like teddies can break. Or, if you set the house on fire... Well, that of course is different 'cause it doesn't matter if it's hard or soft. It just matters how much lighter fluid or gasoline you use. Or both if you have

71

them. Actually, I like fire more than I like soft things, but I don't think I'm supposed to talk about that with you right now. My doctor says that as long as I remember to think of positive things like my teddy—before my Mommy ripped his arms off—then I should be much better real soon. Not that I didn't feel much better after the fire... Well, sorta... That's how I burned my legs. See? I ran back in to get teddy's arms. They were under Mommy's bed and I had to crawl way back under there to get them... I got 'em! Yes, I did. It wasn't easy 'cause my Mommy was yelling at me. "Help me, help me! Please, God, Mark *(or Maria)*, please help me!" And I couldn't concentrate. I didn't think she would yell at me so much this time, but she did... I mean, the curtains were so pretty that way... The fire crawling over things like that... I thought she'd like the colors, you know? I didn't think it would hurt though. It hurt real bad 'cause some of the fire got on me, but my doctor says I'll be better real soon. (Beat) So, yeah... Sally, my nurse, sewed teddy's arms back on and put bandages all over him to help him heal. Now teddy looks just like my Mommy with all of the bandages and stuff. (Beat) Although my Mommy could be hard on me sometimes, well, now that she's like teddy, I know that she'll be real soft from now on... And once my Mommy wakes up again, we'll all go home real soon. Real, real soon. And be soft... and huggable... together... all the time... (Beat) See? Now you know... I like soft things. Soft is good. Hard... is bad.

Who:

Whom:

When:

Where:

What:

Why:

How:

What:

How:

FORGIVENESS

(Our hero speaks to his/her alcoholic mother as he/she stands in the kitchen watching the mother pour another glass of scotch and soda.)

It's not affecting me? You don't think what you're doing is really affecting me? (Beat) It starts first, here ... Yeah, in my fingertips. It moves from my hands to my wrists, and then up my arms. I can feel it, movin', like itchy, electric ants crawling under my skin, over my shoulders and up to my neck... the back of my head, over the top and then down my forehead. It moves through me... over me 'til it reaches my mouth. And just when I can't take it no more, it stops. Just like that, it stops. Weird, ain't it? I told that stupid shrink you make me go to— *"Cause I got issues to sort out"*—Yeah, I told him. Told him that I get electric ants crawlin' in my arms every time I see you drinkin'. Every time. Never fails. (Beat) And I've forgiven you every time. Scratched myself raw, but I've forgiven you. It's a disease, right? A disease that makes you drink and gives me electric ants at breakfast, after school, on weekends at the laundromat, the drive-thru at McDonald's, on our way to Grandma's, to the Food Town and the bank. On the back porch, in the kitchen, in the bathroom, your bedroom mostly... the garage even. You drink everywhere. You like to wander, migrate from room to room with the Scotch. And I've forgiven you 'cause you're all I got. You're all I got and I'm all you've got, and I'm trying to keep it all together, you know? But you keep messing it up! Telling me you're doing one thing and then going out doing another. You're the adult, not me! Why can't I come home to a clean house and cookies baking, or at least the breakfast dishes clean and the dog put out for once? Why can't I be the kid, huh? Why can't I be the kid with sleepovers and birthday pool parties? You haven't baked me a birthday cake since I was five, but I've been making ones for you every year since I was six. Why is that? (Pause) You didn't even notice that I threw out a bunch of booze two nights ago when you went out with your "friends"... So drunk that you thought you drank it all yourself, didn't you? But it didn't make no difference 'cause your *friends* just got you some more. Some friends, man. Some friends they are knowin' you're supposed to be going to AA instead of out to Lucky Duck's on I-80 tossin' back enough to put a herd of elephants down. They're out there getting you messed up every night when you should be home with your kid, Mom, when you should be home with me maybe... helping me with my homework, asking me about my day... what I want to do, what I want to be, and just being here when I need you... just talking to me. Just talking to _me_ for a change, instead of the Scotch and soda, and a bunch of jerks that don't give a damn about you. Do you understand what I'm saying, Mom? Your actions are affecting me. Your drinking is affecting me, and if you understand that—if you do, if you really do—then you'll put the drink down... You'll just put the glass down, take my hand... and talk to me... I'm right here... Just... please, just talk to me. (Beat) ...And I'll forgive you... (Watches as Mom makes the decision to put the glass to her lips and drink; begins to scratch arms and neck. There is only disappointment.)

Who:

Whom:

When:

Where:

What:

Why:

How:

What:

How:

THE NEVER COMING BACK

(Lauren—or Levi—has been standing silently watching his/her siblings argue about their mother abandoning them. When the older sister explains that once she finds her keys, she's leaving and never coming back, Lauren/Levi finally speaks up.)

Lauren/Levi: Out there in the "Never-coming-back", you'll look at them and remember the time we got locked out and you had to come home early from dance to let us in after school 'cause Mom forgot about us again. Or the time we used your house key to win sixty-five bucks off scratchers, and bought Dad a new tie and Mom that cool antique compass... So silly... We actually thought it would help her find her way home on the nights she'd stay out too late. Maybe you'd remember how we strung up the old keys and Mom's bottles and made wind chimes that made the most awesome sounds... Well, until she got mad, yanked them down and smashed all the bottles 'til her fingers bled. You pulled the glass out with tweezers for two hours and she never felt a thing... I don't know... Maybe you just want to forget that part, maybe... Maybe just remember that through all of it, we were here. Together. I was here right along with you when she snuck out and left us... and her keys behind...

Who:

Whom:

When:

Where:

What:

Why:

How:

What:

How:

ACCUSED

(Our hero—or is he/she?—is sitting in an interrogation room at the police station. The cops watch as the father listens to the story again. Note: It is important to choose if this character is guilty or innocent, and make clear choices as to how he or she will explain the events.)

I didn't do it! I'm telling you, it wasn't me. (Beat) What? You have to look at them to get the truth? How would they know? They weren't there, none of them. None of 'em were there so how could they know if I did it? Why can't you just believe me... why can't my word be enough for you? Look me in the eye, huh, look me in the eye. See! I wasn't there! (Pause) Fine. You want it again, huh? Fine. I was doing just like you told me. I left the house at three to pick up Nan... AND I WALKED 'cause you said the car was off limits, remember? She gets out at 3:25, so I left at three on the dot 'cause that's when Springer ends—the show. I walked down Kressel past the park, then took the path through the woods to the Elementary. I brought three snack-cakes with me—two for myself, one for Nan 'cause I was actually gonna be nice to the little dork— that's probably the wrappers they found. I was takin' my time thinking it was only a ten minute walk, you know, just eatin' my snack-cakes. But then I looked at my watch and saw that it was 3:22. So I started running. You know, to get there in time, so I wouldn't hear her mouth about being late again, 'cause I'm sure she'd blab to you as always. And since she's your favorite and you always take her side, I figured I'd better haul a-, I mean, I figured I should run real fast to get there. I know Jeff Garby said he saw me running... Well, that's why. (Beat) I'm telling you, I was running 'cause I wanted to get to Nan in time... that's all. (Beat) I lost the third friggin' snack thing 'cause it probably fell out of my pocket while I was running... It was bloody 'cause...'cause the rip...I remember now... The rip was 'cause my shirt got caught on some sticker bush at the fork in the path and it cut the crap out of my arm—I mean, my hand. The blood was from the cut. See? It's not bleeding like it was then, but I guess I didn't really notice 'cause I was too busy running toward the school. I get there, all out of breath, you know—Mrs. Farmer, the principal, can back me up 'cause she was out there and saw me. I was just three minutes late. I stood out there for like twenty minutes, but Nan never came out. That's when Mrs. Tate, her teacher or whatever comes over to me saying that Nan left on the dot and was walking home...said she saw her walking toward the woods like ten minutes before I made it to the front of the school. (Beat) Mrs. Tate's the one that noticed I was bleeding. She took me to the nurse, you know, but I told her I had to get home before Nan 'cause I didn't know if she had a key. But she insisted. So that was like another twenty minutes. By the time I get back to the path, there's all these cops and an ambulance and all that... Some kid says, they found a little girl in the creek. I didn't even think it was... I mean, how... I just figured Nan was home, sitting on the porch, all ticked off and ready to scream at me—"*I'm telling Daddy! I'm telling Daddy!*"—so I just walked home... took my time 'cause what was the point of getting there... I was already late and she was gonna tell on me anyway. Right? I mean, she always tells, and you always believe her. She can do no wrong, she's perfect... She's God's gift to parents, "Your little angel". Ain't that right? I already knew *the little angel's* wings would be in a bunch, so I took the side streets, stopped into the A&P and got myself some more snack-cakes... I was on my way home when the cops picked me up just down the street. (Beat) That was nine hours ago, Dad. Nine, and you're just now comin' in to see me? Nine hours and you come in here... and the first thing you say to me is what? ADMIT WHAT, DAD? ADMIT WHAT? That I... What? My kid sister? No way...No way, man. Not gonna happen, 'cause I wasn't there. Ask Mrs. Farmer... Ask the nurse, even Mrs. Tate. I was not there! It wasn't my fault! It wasn't... (Beat) But, you know... If anything, it's yours. Yeah, I hate to say it, but if you think about it, it's your fault. If you'da let me drive, I would have gotten there on time and none of this would have happened. None of it. If you just had'a let me drive... Just a bad decision, I guess... A bad punishment for accidentally dinging her stupid bike with the car door... A bad punishment, Dad. Bad. (Beat) Hey, where are you going... Where... Don't. Don't go... I'm sorry. I'm sorry... I shouldn't have said that... I shouldn'ta... Dad! I didn't do it. You've got to believe me... I didn't do it. Dad! Dad! Dad...

Who:

Whom:

When:

Where:

What:

Why:

How:

What:

How:

PART THREE: MONOLOGUES FOR YOUNG WOMEN

THE LEGEND

(Naughty or nice, Molly loves Santa. To death.)

Molly: Oh, my gosh! It's really you... It's you! (Whispering) Oh, yeah... Don't want to wake up Mom and Dad... It's really you! (Whispering) Here, in my own house... Right where I always thought you'd show up; near the tree and just across from the fireplace... Stockings hung by the chimney with care, you know? I had the sugar plum thing going, but then I remembered the cookies. The cookies... I bet you've had enough chocolate chip and oatmeal raisins to last a lifetime... Just the thought of cookies for a lifetime, funny... I mean, I've tried leaving out just about every kind, as you already know... sugar cookies, peanut butter cookies, ones with nuts, ones without... Oreo, Oreo Double Stuff, Chips Ahoy, Mrs. Fields, Sarah Lee, Vanilla Wafers and even Ginger Snaps the one year... Not to mention my Girl Scout phase; I never did see you as a Thin Mint man. And then I thought to myself, why not just go all out, you know? Go the distance! And I was right. Snickerdoodles... I knew you'd like them. Good old fashioned Snickerdoodles... With rice milk, of course. I don't know anyone who would have a problem with rice milk. I mean, soy can be a little heavy, but just imagine having a lactose moment over Greenland... I mean, with your workload and all... (Beat) Almost forgot to put them out... The cookies... Oh, the cookies... Are you ok? Don't worry, it's just Valium... Yes, the sugar mixture on the cookies. It's sugar, cinnamon... and shaved Valium. My mother's... Long story. You'll be fine in a few hours... I'm sorry about, well, having to do it this way, but... You didn't answer my letters, and I was getting worried that we'd never meet face-to-face, and then we moved—I wrote again—but I didn't know if you got the change of address, and I was so worried, and... Anyway... (Beat) How was your trip? Gosh, "How was your trip..." I sound like a nut. Man, I can't believe you're actually here! I always knew this day would come... I remember when I was three, and Mom took me to Macy's just to sit on some impostor's lap. He really was working that fake beard for all it was worth... Even then I knew only the real thing would do. I snatched that beard off his face so fast that he bit his lip, blood started pulsing out of his mouth and spraying all over the other children. Parents were screaming, kids were crying, the elves went on strike... Even fake Rudolph caught on fire. But that was not my fault. Really. Just a happy coincidence, I guess. Anyway... I have the legend of all legends in my house... In a giant butterfly net and doped up on Valium, but a legend none the less... I'm your biggest fan. Really, I am. I know that you know all that is good in my heart. Remember the year that I cut off all my dolly's hair and threw all six pairs of my brother's shoes into the tree? Very naughty. But you still came. The time when I switched the salt with the sugar at Aunt Glady's... She was a diabetic. I was very sorry. But you still came. The week that I was at sleep-away camp and there was that incident with the infestation of fleas and yellow jackets... Again, clearly naughty... But you still came. And I am grateful. Truly. You looked past my faults and still came every year. And although you didn't answer my letters—which does bother me in some way, but I'm sure you have a valid excuse—I must say that your kindness has helped to make me who I am today. And I just wanted to say, finally, face-to-face... I just want to say, Thank you, Santa. I love you. I love you very, very, very, very much. And I know you love me too... (Long pause, then,) No. There was nothing in the milk. Can I get you a pillow? Great...

Who:

Whom:

When:

Where:

What:

Why:

How:

What:

How:

LIKE TOO MUCH INFORMATION

(Isabelle is a very precocious and intuitive Upper East Side Manhattan girl that already knows the dirty little secret her father is hiding, and decides to save her mother the embarrassment of telling it to her.)

Isabelle: I know something's wrong... You only take me on drives in the "country" when something is wrong... And since Central Park is as country as you get, riding back and forth from the East to the West Side usually means it's a big one. And you hate the West Side. (Beat) Okay, I can take it. Tell me your worst. The dog ran away, Grams had a stroke, our apartment is being sublet by Martians... You found out YOU ARE a Martian... No, no... That would mean I'm part alien. Not good for getting into Princeton... Although, it could get me a minorities scholarship to Harvard... (Beat) You're not laughing. Hello? (Sarcastically) Oh, please no, Ma, don't talk to me. No, no, no more. You just talk too much... Stop, it's like too much information. (Beat) You drag me away from cleaning my room after yelling at me about godliness, cleanliness, responsibility, Happy, Dopey, Sleepy, Bashful... Did you know that making your child clean his or her room is actually a form of child abuse? Yes, according to Lizzy

Frinkle's mother, Frances Adolphe Frinkle, it is the worst form of child abuse imaginable. Mm-hm. Gives you low self-esteem AND bad skin... She says that anything that can be done by the maid, <u>should</u> be done by the maid... "Live by the maid, die by the maid" she says... Then again, I saw the maid's face when she said that, and let me tell you, Mrs. Frances Adolphe Frinkle may just get her wish. (Beat) Come on! Tell me! I'm dying here... I mean, okay... Okay already. I was just trying to lighten the mood. You look so worried that even those Botox injections seem to be reversing... No, no they're not. I'm just kidding. Ma! What is it? You're sitting there like a stone... You're scaring the taxi driver. You're scaring me... (Beat) I know what it is. Daddy donated your Saks Card to charity. Humph, no, that would mean he took the time out to actually be home for once. Did you tell him that I've just about forgotten what he looks like? Business, always away on business. How many seminars in Cleveland can one man attend?! Tell me now, Ma. Daddy's a drug dealer, right? You can tell me. He's a drug dealer. Everything is always hush-hush. He's always scurrying around on the phone... His pager going off. All the whispering he does—when he's home! Pot? Cocaine? Heroine? No, not his style... Oh god, it's Rogaine isn't it? Say it, Ma. Daddy is smuggling Rogaine and the feds are after him! Oh! It makes perfect sense! He's a hair sur-geon—plug it here, slap it up there—and now he's had his fill of scalpage and is smuggling Rogaine! I knew it! I knew it! Evil man, Daddy... Evil man for his evil crimes! Abandoning his family to fly to the Rogaine capital of the world—Cleveland—for goodness sakes! God, what will we do if the feds catch him? We'll have to have one of those things, those interventions, right, Ma? That's what they call them, interventions. We'll sit him down and we'll say, "Daddy," Okay, I'll say Daddy, you'll say Walter. Okay, you'll say, "Walter, I'm tired of you being away in Cleveland smuggling your precious Rogaine when I'm here waiting at home for you, when your children are waiting here at home for you... We love you, and although Cleveland offers you something that you "think" is worth more than our love, more than our family, more than what we've built this marriage on, you've got to see that it's tearing us all apart... Your absence is killing us, and we refuse to take it anymore. We refuse to wait for you to remember us... So, you make the decision, Daddy—I mean, Walter—you get yourself together, stop this Cleveland crap, all of your late night phone calls and whispering, and make up your mind. It's either us or her! (Beat) I mean, it's us... or the Rogaine... Yeah, Rogaine or us, Daddy, I mean, Walter. Us or the Rogaine. You decide." (Pause, then finally a smile.) Wow, you're actually smiling... Was getting worried that the Botox had gone a little too deep. (Beat) You ready to go home, or one more time across 79th? Great. Anything's better than cleaning my room. I'm telling you, it's child abuse. I can feel my self-esteem lowering as I speak... Oh, oh God, is this a pimple? See... I told you. Child abuse, Ma. Pure child abuse. (Smiles knowingly.)

Who:

Whom:

When:

Where:

What:

Why:

How:

What:

How:

BUT I CAN'T FIGHT THIS FEELING ANYMORE

(Brianna can't take her mother's shopping obsession anymore!)

Brianna: Step away from the sweater... I'm telling you, just put it down, back away, and we'll go out of here, you and me... together, Mom. Just you and me... No questions. Just put the sweater down. No, no... Stay with me... Stay with me. Listen to my voice, okay? Just listen to me for one time in your life, please, Ma, please. You don't need this. You don't need the sweater... the jeans or the purse... It's not like we haven't gone through this before: Blue Light Special does not mean "Buy everything 'cause one item is on sale." And please, don't look at me like that, Ma. Believe me, I'm not trying to hurt your feelings, I'm just trying to save you some grief... You remember when you took me to Macy's for the white sale and forgot me in the pillow section for six hours? That wasn't a good thing. Yes, I know you only put me down for a minute, Ma. Yeah, I know, but just 'cause you didn't have enough room in your arms or my stroller at the time for all the comforters and sheets, still doesn't make it any better. I know, I know, it was a great sale. Great... I was three, Ma... And it was not exactly a fun ride for me, okay? Or that time you ditched me at the mall for some sale at Zales... Yeah, I know you got a great ring that you'll one day give to me when I get engaged. Sweet thought, Ma. But when did you ever think that leaving a six-year-old in the mall alone for nine hours was a good thing? Yes, I know you'd learned your lesson by then and super glued me to the café chair, but I'll tell ya, that was not exactly a good day for me or my shorts, okay? Any way you look at it, super glue is no babysitter, okay? (Beat) No, I'm not trying to hurt your feelings. I'm not saying you're a bad mother that needs psychological help and a credit card counselor... It's just that look in your eye. It's that look when I know that I've disappeared and whatever is on sale has suddenly become your favorite thing... I'm just tired of looking at marked down prices and feeling jealous, Ma. I'm tired of hearing, "Clean up on aisle five," and fearing that you've fallen between office supplies and ladies fashions... no doubt hurting yourself because you were too busy going for the half-off post-its, slipped on a thong and broken your neck. I just can't see you do this to yourself anymore... Don't you see, I need you. I need you and I know that one day—maybe not today, tomorrow, or even during the clearance sale at Barney's next week—but someday, you'll see that if you just give me some of your time, if you just see past the twenty-five dollars off, buy one get one free fever-feeling, you'll see that I love you, and that I want you to truly see me and not what's on sale. Okay? So, just put the sweater down and we'll walk out of here together... Please. Just put the sweater down. Put it down, Ma. Ma... Put it down. (Beat) Good... No, they don't come in my size. Put it down. Put it down, Ma.

Who:

Whom:

When:

Where:

What:

Why:

How:

What:

How:

MAGNETIC

(As Brandy's best friend, Jackie has to do the right thing and school her on the finer points of what it means to be a woman.)

Jackie: So it's true... You're actually going out with him... Him? Why did I have to hear it from Sarah? Big mouth Sarah... She said she heard it from Chris, who said she heard it from Megan Brice, who said she saw you hold his hand at lunch! You know she told everybody in Ms. Goist's health class, right? Megan, not Chris. Everybody in the world knew but me. (Beat) You weren't gonna tell me, were ya? Man... Just let the grapevine spread the news... Thanks. Guess it makes sense though... I mean, just about every single time Bobby Fritz walks by, you turn three different shades of stupid. "Oh, my gosh, Bobby's coming." "Oh my gosh, Bobby's so cute." "Oh my gosh, Bobby has the deepest dimples. He thinks I'm hot." Are you nuts? It's not cool, Brandy. It ain't cool 'cause you know the only reason he "thinks you're hot" and even talks to you is because of, well, you know... *Those*. Don't act like you don't know. Come on! We all leave fifth grade looking the same, but you're the only one that comes back with those massive things! (Beat) Every woman knows that those things are like magnets for boys. Really. They're magnetic. My sister told me that we— all women, every last one of us—have to watch out for this... It's like a sickness, a disease or something that comes on when boys get to junior high. And having big ones... like

97

yours... well, will attract the nasty of the nasty because those things are just sitting there, up on your chest like signs that say, "Hey, look, I'm out of my training bra, please be a jerk about it!" And that jerk is Bobby Fritz. He's a mental case! (Beat) He's only popular now 'cause he's the only sixth grader that made varsity basketball, but he's the same kid that swiped our Brownie sashes and wore them on his butt in third grade. He's the weirdo that kidnapped Mr. Wiggles in fourth. And everybody knows we loved that hamster... I don't care what you say, Mr. Wiggles' death was not an accident! That boy is the same loser that told everybody that we had finger fungus. Don't you remember? He said he saw me picking my nose after I beat him in the egg toss on Field Day... I was not! But he still ran around like an idiot saying I had finger fungus... "Catchy Finger Fungus" that stuck to you and to anyone that touched us, forever! You said you hated him. <u>We</u> said we'd hate him—together!—forever! And here it is the first week of basketball season and you've had a change of heart because he was the high scorer in last night's game?! You want to be with him? (Beat) Oh, no... No... Don't cry. Please...come on... It's not that I don't want to see you happy, it's just that in cases like this—when a person, a best friend type person, is about to ruin the rest of her life—I have to ask myself, what would I want my best friend to do for me? And that is tell the truth... Dump him. Dump him. Dump him. Okay? Okay... Oh, and what I said about, well... you know, those... Don't worry... Well, my mother says that it gets better after forty... Something about gravity and a man's libido... I don't get it either, but I'm sure it's gotta be better than this.

Who:

Whom:

When:

Where:

What:

Why:

How:

What:

How:

HENRY

(Set in a small town in the mid-1960s, this piece takes place on the roof of a four-story building where Regina's best friend, Henry, is threatening to jump.)

Regina: No, no... Listen to me... Listen to me, please. Don't look at them. No, don't look at them, they don't matter. Please! Please... look at me. I'm telling you it's all... it's all—All of it—it's alright. You don't have to do this. You don't. It's not worth it... We can fix this. Yes, yes we can. WE, Henry. We, just you and me, just me and my Henry. We've been through it all, you and me, right? Am I right? No... no, don't look at them, look at me, right at me, Henry. Forget about them. They don't exist... Nobody but you and me. Just you and me... like the time we went over to Mr. Wilson's Grocery... Yeah, yeah, remember that, Henry? You got the key off your old man while he was asleep in that old Lazy Boy your mom called "The Wagon?" Ha! And I came up with the best plan ever... No one else would have tried it, no one...nobody but you... you believed in my schemes. You believed in me... you always did. (Beat) Just two stupid kids looking for fun, huh? Stealing keys from your tired Pop and sneaking into the grocery on Halloween... You'd think old man Wilson would have had the alarm set, you know? But that old geezer! He'd forget his teeth, his pants that one winter, and the alarm, but he'd never forget to be as mean as he could be to the kids from 'cross the tracks... "Trailer Trash," he'd call 'em, "Just nasty trailer trash." You'da thought he'd put two and two together after we glued all the sweet corn cans together. Ha, remember that? But man... You that Halloween night. You taking every stick of gum, every lollypop, every jawbreaker, every piece of candy you could get your hands on... even the Chiclets! All that candy, and we were outta there... But you said we shouldn't take it for ourselves. No, not my Henry, we took it 'cross them tracks and treated all the kids down there for a night that I'll never forget... Gave it to the kids, the parents even. Yeah, real Robin Hoods we were. And we did it together... (Beat) But you told the cops that it was you, all you, Henry. Told me to keep my mouth shut, and you told the cops that I didn't have a thing to do with it—"How could some girl come up with such a plan?" And they put you in juvie for two months. You went away for two months for me...and I loved you for it, Henry. I loved you then... and I... Henry, please. Listen to me, Henry. Don't look at them! They don't know you like I know you. They don't know what you been through... they don't... (Aside) No! Tell them to step back! I said, tell them to step back! (To Henry) You don't have to do this. Henry, we can fix this. It's just a moment, just a moment, Henry, and this time, this time you don't have to go it alone. I promise... So just come back, come off the ledge, and we'll work it out. You and me, me...and my Robin Hood. Okay? Alright? It's all... it's alright. See? It's alright. (She outstretches her arms to watch him turn to face her. He smiles and speaks to her. She mouths " I love you too", and then...) HENRY! No...no...

Who:

Whom:

When:

Where:

What:

Why:

How:

What:

How:

SAFE

(Ellie suffers from Obsessive Compulsive Disorder. Counting helps, but it isn't easy for her to stay calm while talking to her therapist and receiving treatment as an in-patient in a mental ward.)

Ellie: Three, six, nine... No, no... Don't touch that. No... Please... Man... Now I have to wash my hands again. No! Don't! (Beat) Can I go home now? I don't like it here. Three, six... Don't you think the staff should wear masks? You could at the very least offer masks to the patients. My God, that guy down in C-5 hasn't bathed since I got here. And that redheaded girl! What is with those teeth?! And she keeps picking at herself... Everywhere! Picking, picking, picking... Her parents should be shot! I mean, it's one thing not to teach your child proper hygiene, but her teeth? When she smiles I swear I wanna commit suicide. She's got summer teeth... Sum'er there, sum'er not, and most of them look like they're saluting the flag. How does she eat? I just want to smash her face in! But I'm too scared to touch her... That picking... (Beat) Her skin... It's everywhere. I know it's everywhere. And *they* are every-where, all the time... (Beat) I saw this documentary thing on PBS once. Yeah, there was this scientist that said that there are like billions of them—BILLIONS—floating around, moving around. On everything, on everyone... Three, six, nine... Okay, okay. Yeah, so not only are they out there, in

103

here, around waiting for us, but there are these things, these mites that eat... They live in our beds and the carpets... They eat our flesh. Awh! They eat our dead, flaked-off flesh... Even that redheaded girl's. Apparently, they have no account for taste... (Beat) What do you think it tastes like? Those microscopic flesh sandwiches... Those mites and their little mite lives... Eating, eating, eating... Do they pull up to a bed in their little mite cars and order flesh with fries, a soda... is there special sauce? (Beat) Don't look at me like that... that look. Just like my mother— Edie, Mrs. Edie Fry and her looks... Like *she* knows everything. Do you know what she says to me? My mother—Mrs. Edie Fry—keeps saying, "Don't worry about it... You worry about too much, Ellie...It's not something to worry about." What?! Is she kidding? Hasn't she heard of the plague! One good germ, on one bad flea, on a rat with a little motivation, and we're back in the middle ages, trying to get rid of the stench... Bodies piled up every morning with nowhere to put them, just leaving them on the sidewalks to rot... Half the neighborhood dead and dying before their Fruit Loops get soggy. None of us, none of us will survive... Three, six... Three, six. Nine! (Beat) I'm sorry, I'm sorry. It's just that I don't think this is going to work out. It's just not working out. The mites, the teeth-girl-picking thing... The mites... No masks. Plague... It's just not working out... I just wanna go home... Can't you just let me go home? Please? Three... Please? No, don't touch that. NO! Don't touch me! Please, I just wanna go home where... Three. Where... Three... Where it's, three, six... nine. Safe.

Who:

Whom:

When:

Where:

What:

Why:

How:

What:

How:

MALT-O-MEAL...AND MILLY

(Becky is stuck in the house watching her little sister Milly. Again! And Milly just loves to ask, "Why?")

Becky: For God bless American cotton, Milly! Shut the heck up! You talk and you talk and you talk like you know everything and the more you talk the more I wanna call the nearest rehab center and enroll, or whatever! Geez! I don't even do drugs, but you make me wanna! Shut up. Oh, now you're crying. Whatever. Do you want the Frosted Flakes or the Malt-O-Meal? You know you want the friggin' Malt-O-Meal... Because I gave you a choice. It's good to have choices... Because that's how the world works. Because that's what Mom and Dad said before they left me in the house with you. Because they are insane. Because they didn't put you up for adoption. Because I don't know how to make your random death look like an accident! Ask me why again and I'll figure it out. (Beat) So... Question: Frosted Flakes or the Malt-O-Meal. (Beat) I thought so.

Who:

Whom:

When:

Where:

What:

Why:

How:

What:

How:

THE ELEPHANT IN THE ROOM

(Georgia has watched way too many Lifetime movies. So when her folks tell her that they "need to get things aired out," Georgia takes it to a whole new level.)

Georgia: Ok, so let me get this straight, 'cause I'm doing everything I can to not explode when we all know that there is a huge elephant in the room... Come on! You just said that you "need to get things aired out." Mom's going to Aunt Regina's for four weeks, and you're going to stay at the condo until we get back from camp. Right? The twins are going with Mom after camp and you want me to come stay with you until "things get aired out." Right. That's what you said: "Until things get aired out." (Beat) Ok. Would someone please tell me what LIFETIME MADE FOR TV MOVIE you people are smoking?! OMG! (Beat) Is it me, or do you really think this is going to end well? This NEVER ends well. Ok. See... Right now I'm having the "angst-y teenage outburst"—I squabble and whine about how "things getting aired out" is really code for separation and divorce, and vainly try to remind you that we were once a special family. I scream how you can't do this to me, how all my other friends' parents are divorced and now they are in counseling or in need OF counseling... I cry and plead to you about how things will never be the same and that you have ruined my life because I was one of the very few real teens that believed in love, the sanctity of marriage, and really thought I had amazing parents. THEN! I start to cry harder! You try to comfort me, but not before I vow to run away. I bound up the stairs. Softly, we hear the twins crying in the corner of the room as I turn my back and slam the door behind me. Close-up of my tear stained cheeks... You go to embrace the twins as they moan in the agony of disappointment while I gather my things— the teddy Mom gave me in fouth grade and the bracelet Dad bought me when I got my braces. I pack them in my backpack, slip out the window, onto the roof, down the side of the house and disappear into the woods. I look back with sadness and disdain just as we cut to a commercial about ready-made hot-wings... We come back, and FIFTEEN YEARS LATER, YOU'RE STILL LOOKING FOR ME! But I've become a beggar, a hobo, a wayward woman looking for the next place to hide from The Man. By now, I've lost an eye in a bar fight over a bad con job and a boy named Luke that left me for a dirty blonde and a German Shepherd with a limp. Yes. See, I'm a worn out, one-eyed hustler trying to make my way on the streets of Juno, Alaska! Just trying to make a buck in the cold, dark and lonely night, backlit by the Aurora Borialis, of course... The patch over my eye, my only steady companion... And then, THEN!, when you've given up on me, just when you've decided to give up the search and throw in the towel, you realize that it has been your love for me, your love for one another and this family that has given you the strength to search—YOU

MOM, AND YOU DAD! TOGETHER!—just one more time. And on the coldest of Juno nights, you find me under a bridge. You wave. I see you together. Joy abounds, and as we cross to one another, we all remember this very day, the day that tore us apart, but now one that brings us together... You run to me and me to you, and just as I make my way across a frozen pond and you across the highway... I'm run down by a sled team of twelve huskies and an Eskimo grieving over the loss of his family fortune and his dead pet moose. The very fortune and moose he lost because of the bad con job! (Beat) You see? You see? It's not a good ending, people! Not for any of us. Me. You... the Eskimo.... He's lost someone too, you know? And you can't blame him because I didn't see him coming! Eye patch, remember?! Eye patch. But it's just pathetic that it had to happen in the first place! Don't you see that "letting things air out" is not the way to do this! We have to stick together! You have to work this out, Mom! You have to put in the work, Dad! Think! Please (Pause) Wait... What do you mean "we just have a big termite problem?" We just have a, what? You're calling in an exterminator for the termites and you don't want us to inhale the fumes?? We need to "air things out"... (Long pause, inhale, long exhale.) OK. (She quickly walks away.)

Who:

Whom:

When:

Where:

What:

Why:

How:

What:

How:

WHEN LIFE GIVES YOU LEMONS

(Andrea talks to the new girl on the block about how cutthroat the competition is for Best Lemonade Stand. She's wearing an apron and holding a wooden spoon.)

Andrea: Ok. So... You're the new girl, right? My mom says that you folks moved here from Michigan? Right, right. Well, I would say welcome to the neighborhood and welcome to San Diego, but what I really need to say is welcome to the underbelly of the cutthroat world of summer lemonade stands. Yeah, yeah... I could say all the nice stuff about this block—all the kids are cool, all the parents are double cool, our school is cool, the teachers are great... Yadda-yadda-yadda. But it's July. And you moving here in July sets you up for some real catching up to do, OK? Wait. What's your name again? Brittany? Ok, well, Brittany. I'm Andrea, but everyone calls me Andy. And I run my Andy's Dandy Lemonade Stand right here, as you can see. This is my territory, my spot, my locale... My biz-nazz... And like every other gal around here, we have a lemon tree in our backyard. But unlike most gals, *I have* the best lemons in town. Hands down THE BEST. And every year, I win the neighborhood taste test. (Beat) Now, I won't lie. The people that lived here before you—Wendy and her family—they were nice people. Cute older brother, the dad liked to jog with my dad, Wendy's mom was on the PTA with my mom, Wendy and I would hang and do the BFF thing during the school year... But during the summer?! All bets were off, babe. Yeah, they have a nice little lemon tree, which I guess is yours now, but they didn't know how to really take care of it. And their lemonade? Weak. Just a watered down version of slightly yellow water with no real flavor, no heart... No soul. Just sad. But, they were the best competition in town. All these other wannabe's—Alyson Farmer over there, Gabby Weinstart over there, and Lily Haughner up the block—no competition what so ever. But they try and try each year. Poor things... They try so hard, with their sprigs of lavender, their extra lemon rinds and essence of orange, their agave syrup and touch of mint. One year, Gabby even tried brown sugar <u>for goodness</u> <u>sakes</u>! What is she mad? It's lemonade! Not some kind of science experiment here people! It's just water, ice, sugar and lemons. Simple. And that's how I do it. And THAT'S how I've been making this stand work for the last five years. I respect the lemon, baby. Respect the lemon and the lemon will respect you. That's right. Just easy-peasy-lemon-squeezy... But now? With you in the 'hood, well, I'm looking for some real competition. Some of that mid-western flavor to spice it up this summer, you know? And I'm hoping you got what it takes to take it all the way. Really. I want you to bring it. I want you to serve up your best, your top of the heap yellow elixir, and serve it, baby. I want you to give me a run for my twenty-five cents a cup. I want you to bring the heat. Because believe me, I'm packin' and I ain't packin' light. So? What do you say there, Brittany? You got what it takes? You ready for the heat? (Beat) Oh? Oh??? Really? No way? Really? You're allergic to lemons? Can't even touch them? Darn! (Beat) Well... I guess that means we're gonna be best friends! Well, until the fall when we all start baking brownies for the neighborhood bake off... But that's not for a while. So here, have a seat, I'll pour you a glass of water...

Who:

Whom:

When:

Where:

What:

Why:

How:

What:

How:

HAMLET

(Charlotte has grown up in the shadow of her father's successful acting career, and his addiction. It has taken a toll on their relationship, and she's finally ready to confront him.)

Charlotte: Wait, wait. Let me get this straight. You want <u>me</u> to give a little. You want me to... You know what? For about five seconds—just five seconds, I actually believed you. No, really, I did. That part about you loving me and wanting us to be closer, and that everything will work out as long as you and I work together. That was good, real good. You even seemed sincere with that quivering lip and the watery eyes bit—no tears, but just a hint of them, just the essence of a tear to give the moment a little "something", a little je ne sais quoi. That was good. You really are a professional. I'm proud of you, Dad. I mean, wow. I always thought standing in the wings watching you do your work was a privilege. Othello, Macbeth, Hamlet—now that was a proud moment... The president and his family there in the audience watching my Dad be tortured and Danish. Holding my breath... So proud, so proud. Happy for you that the President of the United States, his wife and children, were fourth row center watching you—watching you tear down your mother, detest your uncle, abandon your friends—as stupid as they are anyway—and play with the emotions of a girl that adored you, loved and needed you... and kill her father and brother to boot. And in the end everyone gets poisoned, right? What would a tragedy be without a little poison? What do you think they used, a little cocaine here, a little heroin there... some meth in the night shade? No. No, that's a little too modern for that play, a little too close to what was already running through your veins that night. (Beat) But they'd love you anyway. They loved you that night. All of them. Everyone. And they had no clue. The critics, the President, his wife and their kids... No clue. On their feet after everyone gets poisoned, cheering, screaming my daddy's name. 'Cause at the end you get to come back from the dead—night after night, after night—you come back from the dead, shake off the night's drama, and take a bow. (Beat) Well, take a bow, Daddy. (Clapping) Go ahead. Shake off the drama—the broken promises, the "no, no, pumpkin, I'll be there, don't you worry," the fights with Mom when she could still stand to be in this house with you, the nights, hell, the weeks that you didn't come home—the performances were over but you just couldn't—no, <u>wouldn't</u> come home... Shake it off, Daddy, and take a bow. Shake it all off. But remember, I was there to see you die. I saw my father die every night on cue, but as far as I'm concerned—<u>Daddy</u>—you've never been alive. (Pause) Wow. Incredible... Just look at that. Now those tears actually look real. Impressive. You should get a Tony for that...

Play. Speak.

Who:

Whom:

When:

Where:

What:

Why:

How:

What:

How:

THE READER

(Valerie finally tells her parents what's been bothering her.)

Valerie: Bothering me? You want to know what's bothering me? (Beat) Heaven help us all if Gayle gains weight and can't fit her dresses, or Trish stops working out, puts on a ton and can't play, and Donna stops eating "brain food" and starts pigging out on Ho-Ho's... What then? They'll all end up like Val, "The Reader." That's what's bothering me. You always introduce me with, "...And, Valerie is our reader." Gayle is the beauty queen, Trish is the jock, Donna is the genius, and Valerie is "Our Reader." Four girls... Three with clear-cut talents... The youngest? "Reader." (Beat) I'M FAT, PEOPLE! I'm fat! Just say it! That's my category! My category is <u>clearly</u> all over me, but you say "reader". And you whisper it! You whisper it just like you did when Gramps got sick. *"Prostate cancer."* I don't even have a prostate! But you whisper anyway. *"Reader... AND she has a great personality."* Everybody knows that "great personality" is the code for FAT! It's bad enough that I gotta put up with people asking about Gayle and her pageants, "Gees, Gayle won Teen Miss Ohio? Your parents <u>must</u> be proud...Wow. Donna got a full ride to Oxford? Man, your parents must be proud. Trish was scouted by Arizona? Your parents must be proud!"... And just like that, I can see it in their eyes, "Your parents must be SO proud...<u>of them</u>... But what the hell happened to you, Val?" They look at me like they can't believe that we're even related. And that's the exact same look you two have when you introduce me to people. Did it ever occur to you that I do more than eat and read? Does it look like I've got *The Grapes of Wrath* spackled to my forehead, or does my size embarrass you so much that you have to make me the next spokesperson for Hooked-on-Phonics and come up with some label—some talent that would only stand out in Appalachia? (Beat) I'm fat, Mom. I'm fat, Dad, and as much as these extra ninety pounds freaks you out, I'm proud of who I am and what I'm about. Just because I'm not into tiaras and sports, or making the mini-van look like The-My-Kid-Made-Honor-Roll-Bumper-Sticker-Fairy puked on it, doesn't make me worthless... or "The Reader." If anything, it makes me stand out from the rest of the crowd... Just like my sisters.

Who:

Whom:

When:

Where:

What:

Why:

How:

What:

How:

PRETTY MUCH THE TRUTH

(Bunny has made it to the finals of the Miss Teen America Pageant. All that's left to do is answer the final question... Truthfully, of course. Note: It is important to make a clear choice about Bunny's character and motives. Is she clueless and just spouts off the truth as best that she can, or is she ruthless and knows exactly what she's doing?)

Bunny: Would you please repeat the question, Bob? (Beat) Thank you, Bob. (Beat) "What does the truth mean to me?" Well, that's a very deep question. And I would first like to say, that the truth is something that my mother—as she always says—sets us free. And freedom, especially in this country, is exactly what this nation was built on. And! It is because of the truth of this nation that young women such as myself and all the beautiful young Miss Teens from around our great nation can pride themselves in standing on as well. I mean, just last night Miss Teen Texas and I were talking about how well Miss Teen West Virginia took constructive criticism and didn't wear that god-awful blue evening gown tonight, and instead went with the black one that better hides the top of her Spanx. Wow. Oh, and just the other day, when Miss Teen Indiana was caught with an illegal tanning device, she didn't hide it nor deny it. And as you can see tonight, she held her head high despite her orange arms and pasty legs. Yes, truth goes a long way. It's tops in my book. Just like Miss Teen Utah's mother who was honest about dating one of the judges last year and didn't send another gift basket to the sponsors of our new bathing suit manufacturers, Ittsy-Bittsy Teenie-Weenies. Now that's truth for you. I personally think it's courageous to tell the truth when it could easily cost you your self-worth, dignity or, more importantly, your crown. I mean, if it weren't for the original Miss Teen Ohio coming forth and telling the truth about all the plastic surgery—the rhinoplasty, liposuction, ear-pinning, veneers, hair extensions, and the tapeworm—I wouldn't be here today. And believe me, I love my sister. Thank you, Brenda. Anyway, it is no wonder that this long-standing pageant is built on, no, fortified by, the truth of what it really means to be a girl. No, to be a pretty girl—with all of your original, god-given parts—and to be ready to win a scholarship for just those parts. Because the truth is that in our beautiful nation and society, it's not just about what you know, or who you are, or even where you want to go in life... No, the truth is: Can you make it look good while you're doing it? And I'd have to say, Bob, with no hesitation, yes I can! And! I can do that and one day create world peace. And that's the truth. Thank you.

Who:

Whom:

When:

Where:

What:

Why:

How:

What:

How:

LAST BEAUTIFUL GIRL

(Laura confronts her sister, Donna.)

Laura: Yeah, I know you love me. Yeah! I know you love me, but would you just stop it? Stop it, stop it! Stop trying to make it all better! (Beat) You can't help it? What can't you help? That you just have to do everything for me? That you have to get me up and out of bed? That you have to help bathe me, wash my hair... Wash my clothes, fold them... You have to cook all of my meals; cut my food like I'm a three-year-old: "Come on, now... Open wide..." Please! I know I may not "seem" whole. My body may "seem" asleep, this or that part may not feel like every-one else "feels", but I'm not helpless! I THINK THEREFORE I AM! RIGHT? Am I right? <u>I think</u>! Okay? And I think it's about time that you get a hobby 'cause I am not it. I am not. And I am not your excuse for not having a life of your own. Don't deny it, I heard you on the phone: "Sorry, Jake. Can't go out 'cause someone has to stay with Laura." "No, no, sorry everybody, I can't meet you there 'cause someone has to clean up after Laura, make sure she gets her meds... make sure she feels like an invalid," and an excuse for every single thing you are running away from... Everything you're hiding from. And you think that because you literally push me around that you can emotionally push me too? You don't get it do you? (Beat) You are the world's biggest flirt. Yeah, flirt. You roll me down Main Street every Sunday after mass, pretending that we're just out for a stroll...Just pushing me around, huh? Letting every guy you see compare us... Yeah, they feel sorry for you. "That poor baby-blue blonde... You can see *she's* the last beautiful girl in her house." I see it in their eyes as they pass. All of them... Even Jake. You roll me down the sidewalks so I can be your two-wheel neon sign. "Look everybody, I've got a sister in a wheelchair, and you should know that I'm sacrificing my all for her... My future, my happiness..." You toss your head back and swing your hair so much, I'm amazed you haven't given yourself whiplash! And that giggle! What is with that giggle? If Mama were alive...(Beat) But she's not... And no matter what I do, I can't make you see that no one blames you for it. It's not your fault. It's not your fault, Donna. And this? Me? It's not your fault either. If any one's to blame it's that damn drunk driver... and maybe being in the wrong place at the wrong time... I may be in this chair, but at the very least I haven't given up on what really counts... You are my sister. But you are not my every-thing... And I've never expected you to be just because you were driving the car that night... Don't you know, that's not part of the "sister contract". (Beat) So go on... Live your life. Live it. I'll be fine... I'll be fine 'cause I know what I've got... I've got you, but most of all, I've got me... I'm not broken. And I'm gonna make it no matter what... And that means from now on, on every Sunday after mass, I'm gonna roll myself <u>up</u> Main Street... (Smiling) You can giggle all you want, Donna... But folks are gonna see that maybe, just maybe, you're not the last beautiful girl in this family after all...

Who:

Whom:

When:

Where:

What:

Why:

How:

What:

How:

SINKING SALLY

(A disappointed Jamie confronts her brother after she fails the lifeguard test.)

Jamie: How did it go? You're asking me now? You're asking me now how did it go? I asked you I don't know how many times to help me count out how many compressions per breaths, or was it breaths per compressions? Or whatever! I asked you to help me for like two weeks to count out the number of breaths and the number of compressions we were supposed to do. But no! No! Would you help me? No! You could have warned me! But now?! Now?! (Pause) You know, it's one thing to be clumsy. I get that. I'm not good at rollerblading or skateboarding. That's all you all the time all summer. You can do that in your sleep. I'm not good at sports that require a ball; football, basketball, kickball, bowling—is that a sport? Tennis, raquetball, golf, lawn bowling, or cricket—which is like weird because it's just baseball with English people that refuse to run any way but back and forth, so you know I'm no good at that... That, or basketball. Whatever! Again, all you! But the one thing, the very one little, tiny, itty-bitty thing that I can do that would actually make a difference, is swimming. And you knew that being a lifeguard means the world to me. That's all I wanted this summer, but no! Just learn CPR. Just learn CPR. (Beat) You could have told me that they give you a fake person. Fake people! Fake, latex people, with no arms or legs! Just a latex head and torso! And you KNOW I'm allergic to latex! I hate you. I hate you, I hate you... (Pause) I couldn't even touch the Sally Doll. She died. She drowned AND THEN SHE DIED! SHE WAS MADE OF LATEX, SHE DROWNED AND THEN I WATCHED HER DIE ON THE SIDE OF THE POOL!... along with all my hopes of ever being a lifeguard. (Beat) I'm gonna go float now... but just want you to know that it's because of your insensitivity and lack of true understanding and just plain love that I will forever blame you—and Mom's bad genes—for my failing the CPR test. (Beat) I would drown myself, but I just found out that the paramedics use latex gloves. I guess I'll have to live... or take up origami this summer. Either way. I'm very, very, very, very... Upset.

Who:

Whom:

When:

Where:

What:

Why:

How:

What:

How:

NOT ALAINA

(Katrina and her mother are at a cousin's birthday party. Kat recently returned home from a treatment center for being a cutter, and is being sequestered with her mother in an adjacent room. Unfortunately, Kat is feeling the anxiety rise while watching her cousin blow out birthday candles, and she's beginning to lose her grip.)

Katrina: What am I supposed to say? What do you want me to say, huh? You're gonna send me back there aren't you? You're gonna ship me back there anyways, so what's the point? (Beat) Why'd you even bring me here?! For her? For cousin Alaina? She doesn't even want me here! She can't even stand the sight of me... None of the family can. Yes, it is true. Look at them. They don't even want me here. No, they don't! (Beat) No, you be quiet! You keep it down! (Beat) Fine, fine... (Pause) Look at her... She's so beautiful. Alaina is so beautiful, isn't she? Ha! Look at all her friends... All those stupid girls and their perfect little view of the world... or how it should be. They don't have a clue. Look at them. (She mocks their laughter.) She's too good for them. Stupid whores. They'll all go and get knocked up by their dumb jock boyfriends... and be fat housewives with two and a half fat kids, with no clue how to love and be just as clueless about how to end it all the right way. But not Alaina... She'll get outta here and go around the world, and be something and be somebody and be what nobody ever thought she'd be because she's the best thing that ever happened to this place. Yes I took my meds!!! No! Don't shush me! You wanted me to come, so here I am and so here I am! All of me and your dark secrets and your shamefaced expressions... You don't see me. You got your eyes looking away when people walk by... Yeah, I see them smile at you like they know what you've been through. Like they know what *you've* been through! Like you're God's gift, like you've gone through some kind of transformation when I'm the one with the scars. (Holds out her wrists.) Look. Look! Look! (She looks at the scars.) I can't even do that right. (Beat) And you can't love me... and I can't stop this anymore. Look. Look what I did, Ma. Look what I did... (Beat) Alaina is so pretty. The prettiest cousin ever. All those candles...(Singing) Happy birthday to you, Happy Birthday to... you...

Who:

Whom:

When:

Where:

What:

Why:

How:

What:

How:

Convincing him of your hurt.

SWEET SIXTEEN

(Julianna confronts her estranged father on the lawn outside of her sixteenth birthday party.)

Dare   *+ taunt*

Julianna: Geez... Leaving again, huh? (Beat) You know... They tell you that this is supposed to be the time of your life, like this is supposed to be the best part of breathing or the best part of having your eyes open or somethin'. *provoke* Eyes open, Eyes open to see what? To see you standing even farther away from me? To watch you walk out while I'm blowing out my candles? To watch you make such a big deal of the presents you bought—some stupid tube socks and a second-hand watch with a busted second hand—just to watch you smoke a cigarette across the street and try to drive off without saying goodbye? (Beat) I thought you quit. You did. You said you quit. Just like you quit us, right? Just like you quit me... (Beat) You wanna know why I invited you? Really? You wanna know why? Because I wanted you to see me cry. Look, Jimmy. Look. I'm crying... You missed it the first time you walked out on us, so I wanted to make sure you were here for my big girly birthday to finally see the tears you missed when you walked out the first time. You missed all the big fat ones and the crocodile ones, and the ones that I swear disappeared just as fast as I pushed them out for you... Or was it as fast as you pushed me out of your life? I don't know... Guess it doesn't matter anyway.

(Beat) Guess all that matters is if you got legs to carry you far enough away so you don't have to watch the people you love blow it, huh? Sixteen candles on my birthday cake... How ironic. Well, you blew it, Jimmy! <u>You blew it</u>! I thought these tears were for you, but now I realize they're for everybody that has ever known your sorry ass. They're for every person that has ever seen your sorry face, that has ever waited to see you after ten years, or even wondered if they'd ever get the chance to say, "Hey, it's OK. I forgive you. We can start over." But you blew it. Just as quickly as I blew out my own stupid candles and you walked away from a perfectly good party... You walked away from a perfectly good chance to know me again, and you blew it. (Pause) So, I just want you to know that. (She backs away.) No. Don't touch me. You don't get to touch me. No, 'cause all you get is to be out here in your stupid truck and remember what it was like to watch <u>me</u> walk away from you this time. You get to watch me walk away. (Turns, pauses, then turns to Jimmy.) You know, in the movies, the girl would say something really clever about how she loved her father—her *Dad*—and how she hoped he'd see her through the next best years of her life, but since you haven't been that man—since you're just the asshole that walked out on us—I'll just say you should keep smoking, Jimmy... I hear those things'll kill ya. (She walks away.)

Who:

Whom:

When:

Where:

What:

Why:

How:

What:

How:

THE EDGE OF THE WORLD

(Gabby—an aspiring actress—takes her craft very seriously.)

Gabby: It is so not right to tell kids that... so not right... I mean, what you're telling us is that the universe—our universe—is expanding, and that one day—some random, maybe sunny or partly cloudy, even snowing if you're on the East Coast... Well, on that random day, the universe will just *swthoop!* Contract... and be less than the size of a spec of dust... A little bit of nothing, formless and tiny just hanging out with nothing to do but expand again. That in itself is terrifying... I mean, with all our other pressures—family, friends, the search for the perfect prom dress—you lay this on us? I mean, just because you have a so-called degree in this, you can't just go around teaching it to young, impressionable kids that already have the world on our shoulders, high expectations from our parents, and unbelievable social pressures and stuff... Let alone this silly notion of the universe collapsing... Please... I mean, let's look at the facts... If the universe were expanding—like you say it is—then why can't I feel it? No, really? I mean, I feel many things in a day: Hatred that stupid Lauren Grazer is squad captain this year; Depression that she's seeing my ex; Fear because they may actually one day marry and populate the world with their evil spawn; Happiness that one day I <u>will</u> be a famous actress, win an Oscar, Tony, Golden Globe, SAG Award...MTV Movie Award or whatever that will make my ex feel like crap for dumping me for that stupid Lauren... Anyway... I don't "feel" the universe expanding. And even if I did, I do <u>not</u> think it would feel the way I am feeling right now. (Beat) Do you know what I am feeling right now? Yes, I am an actress with deep and meaningful feelings that must be unveiled with conviction within the parameters of a given moment... And, as my acting coach says, I must feel it with my entire instrument ablaze from the fire in my belly... But what I am feeling, which is almost indescribable, is this feeling of not enough space for expressing myself, you know? And that, as my mother says, is the fault of a public high school education... I'm only a junior for goodness sakes! Oh, my gosh... The room is spinning... Oh, my gosh... Oh, my gosh... Could it be that because I am so in touch with my feelings and with, possibly the universe, that I am actually feeling... Oh my gosh, could it be that I am actually feeling the universe collapsing right now? Could it? I mean, I'm feeling very... Very... Very...You know, right now? This is awful! This could be the last day of our lives... The edge of the world, the edge of the universe for heaven's sake, could be right in this very classroom... Shrinking around us, moving toward destruction and nothingness... Empty. OH MY GOD! WE'RE ALL GONNA DIE! I CAN FEEL IT! I CAN FEEL IT IN MY BELLY, RIGHT NOW! Feel this, feel my belly... Don't you feel it? Oh... no... Oh, no... Oh, no... Wait. Wait... Then again, it just could be those two double-vanilla lattes

I had for lunch... Hm... Yeah... yeah, I think that's it... Wait. Let me see if I'm feeling the feeling again. (Long pause) Yeah. It's alright... So, like I was saying... You can't go on teaching this kind of stuff without actual proof. It only messes with kids' heads... I mean, not mine because I'm more in touch with my feelings. But with these poor other kids with fewer extracurriculars that keep them out of touch with their feelings, well, it's just not right. It's just *so* not right...

Who:

Whom:

When:

Where:

What:

Why:

How:

What:

How:

PROCRASTINATION

(Raina hasn't completed her science report and has the excuse of ALL excuses. Note: Make a clear choice: Is Raina telling the truth or is she fibbing?)

Raina: It's not that I just didn't do it. I tried. I really did. No, really. I swear, like, I was just about to sit down and write the thing, but then my grandmother called to say that my Uncle Gretchen—it's a long story—was in town, well, in town at that very moment and at the bus station, and Gramsie—that's what we call her, my grandmother, not my Uncle Gretchen—well, Gramsie's car wouldn't start, so someone had to go pick her up, my grandmother, not my Uncle Gretchen. What I mean is, Gramsie wanted to be there when we picked up Uncle Gretchen, so someone had to go pick Gramsie up first and then go get Uncle Gretchen at the bus station—which made no sense because Gramsie lives twenty miles in the other direction, so turning around to come all the way back to the bus station—which, as you know, is only a ten minute drive from our town—was, like, a pain... but anyway... I'm sure my Dad would have just gone over there on his own, you know to get her, but my brother was on a date with that stupid Kristen Summers—yeah, I know!—And like the only car around was mine, and it's a stick. No problem, right? But no, my Dad broke his leg last

Thursday at that indoor climbing wall at Jake's Gym... Did you hear about that? Yeah, he was almost at the very top when the cable snapped—which is like weird 'cause they're made to, like, never snap... It was a nasty fall. Nasty... And so sad, you know, 'cause like, he's acrophobic—fear of heights—and was going there to get over it, 'cause his therapist was like, "You've got to do it to beat back the fear and stuff." So he was climbing for the first time, and snap! It was on the news. My Dad's suing for like a billion dollars. So, anyway, so I'm the only one that can drive—'cause my Dad's like on Tylenol with Codeine. Or is it Valium? No, no it's Demerol, or some whacked out stuff that makes him see God or something fifteen minutes after he takes it. I'm telling you, it was a nasty fall. So, anyway, I had to put down my books and notes to help my family, you know? And I was really mad. 'Cause I was like so into writing it, and had made all of those notes, and the outline, and all that stuff and I was totally into focusing in on the task at hand. So, basically the whole time I was driving, I swear, I was thinking about plate tectonics and their impact on the world as we know it. I kept thinking, man, the plates move and the world shifts, and suddenly, there are new continents and volcanoes... I mean, the Earth could just open up, shift and bam! I kept thinking that at any moment there would be an earthquake and I would be killed just before I got to Gramsie's. Which was probably a bad thing 'cause just ten miles from Gramsie's, I got pulled over by some garlic breath cop that said I was doing eighty-seven in a fifty. Not good, 'cause they'll take your car if you're a minor in this county. Which is exactly what happened! The stink breath cop took me to the station! He said he was tired of "these no account kids getting away with murder," and that he'd had it up to here with our shenanigans. *Shenanigans*? Like, who the heck talks like that?! I had to spend six hours in lockup 'cause my father was stoned on the couch and wouldn't answer the phone, and my brother stayed out way past curfew. Gramsie couldn't help me, 'cause like I said, she's the one that needed the ride in the first place. I got a $150 ticket, my car is impounded, I have to go back to drivers ed *and* attend anger management classes—I'm telling you, I was really upset that I couldn't write my paper last night— and for all I know Uncle Gretchen is still waiting at the bus station wondering where the heck everyone is. (Pause) With that said, I'd like to have another extension on my paper. Please, I just need another week so I can get myself together. I'm sure I'll have my car by then and my Dad'll be off his meds, so if Gramsie calls or my Uncle Gretchen needs a ride, he can drive—my Dad, not Uncle Gretchen. Okay? Really? Great. I knew you'd understand.

Who:

Whom:

When:

Where:

What:

Why:

How:

What:

How:

NOT G. I. JANE

(Vanessa confronts her father during a Father/ Daughter event at the army base.)

Vanessa: Yes, it's true, and I don't see what the big deal is. I know what I want, I know who I am, I know what I'm about and I know what I want to do with my life. So that's it, that's that, and you and what "army" are gonna stop me? (Beat) It's not like I'm not gonna get an education, and it's not like I'm not going to be using my life to serve a higher purpose. Millions of people graduate from high school and go into the Army. Millions of them do that. That's not me, Dad. That was you. And we lived all around the world, in nineteen houses, I went to fourteen different schools, and had, like, two friends, Dad. Two! The first one was imaginary, remember? I do. Mom does. My shrink did. And so did my second friend because he was friends with the first one! So don't tell me that what I want to do with my life is somehow not up to par with a life in the Army! (Beat) Come on! Do you even know what you're saying? Do you? You're saying that you'd rather I'd take up arms and go kill for my country—probably kill more innocent people than terrorists—than take up my cross and follow Jesus?! What the heck? (Beat) No. I said "heck", and you know it. So please, don't even go there. (Beat) I want to be a nun, Dad. And I'm going to be a nun, and you're just gonna have to suck it up. (Beat) Look, you can't just keep following me around the hor dourves table and expect me to change my mind, Dad. I won't, I won't, I won't, I won't, I—OK, and you know what? Then pray about it. Maybe the good Lord will help you see the bigger picture and find peace within yourself. Because heaven help me and heaven help us all if you keep following me around this table.(Beat) Because I don't look good in green, Dad. Because I don't want to have to carry a gun. OK? Because I don't want to have to choose between my life and someone else's. Why? Why? You really want to know why?! BECAUSE I DON'T WANT TO BE YOU! (Pause) I don't want to have to move every few months; pack up my life and all my love just as I was making ties and have to say goodbye. I don't want to have to fight my way out of every situation and fight my way back in just to make a friend, but still be on the outside. I don't want to have my family wait for me for years, just to learn that I can't love anything or anyone up close because all I know is how to strategically bomb people I will never know, never see, nor ever mourn... but still have more pride in wiping them out than wiping my own daughter's tears. So, no. I don't want to be in the Army, Dad. I've had enough of the Army life, I'm fatigued. I'm tired of being camouflaged by its demands. And, heck, you don't see me anyway... You never did. (Beat) So, are we good here? Are we good? Good. And please, be a good soldier and say grace before you eat that pig in a blanket. Have some respect for the man upstairs. He kept you from getting your ass blown off for all these years. And yes, I said ass. For your information, Jesus rode one on His way into Jerusalem. (Beat) And yes, He loves you too.

Who:

Whom:

When:

Where:

What:

Why:

How:

What:

How:

LAST HURRAH JOHN

(Beth finds her brother John hiding in the men's room of the church after a huge secret is revealed just before his wedding.)

Beth: John? John? Where... There you are... (Aside) I shouldn't even be talking to you. (Beat) After what you did... God, you are such a hypocrite! How could you do something like this, John? And on your wedding day?! Ew! John! What the hell! (Beat) Look at me. Look at me! Did you do it? Did you? I'm your sister, John. Geez. Just tell me the truth, did you...? With Laura's sister? (Beat) Oh my god, John! What is wrong with you?! That's like the sacred friggin' holy grail of all sacred friggin' holy friggin' grails, John! Even the ring bearer knows that and he's three-years-old! For the love of Pete Sampras, what were you thinking? (Beat) Last hurrah? You wanted a last—You know what? You've gotten your last hurrah, idiot. Laurie is out there bawling her eyes out because of your "last hurrah". Mom and Dad are trying to keep Laurie's Dad and brother from ripping your throat out because of your "last hurrah". And the rest of the bride's maids have run Laurie's sister into the pastor's study and are trying to break the stinking door down because of your "last hurrah". (Beat) Do you love her, John? Do you love Laurie?! (Beat) Well?! Well?! Unless you want to spend the rest of your life in the men's bathroom reminiscing about the most stupid move you've ever made and the girl you lost, and how you punked out and didn't do everything under God's blue sky to win her back, then I suggest you get out there and fix this. You fix this, John. Get off your butt and you fix this! (Pause) Good. Now stop crying and wipe your nose. Nobody likes to punch snot.

Who:

Whom:

When:

Where:

What:

Why:

How:

What:

How:

THE SPEED OF SOUND

(Cassie is taking her drivers test... AGAIN.)

Cassie: Hi. Nice to meet you too... (Beat, smiling.) That's so funny. I saw Mr. Brock over there and thought that he'd be with me again this time, but... Well, I guess it doesn't really matter who, or is that whom? I don't know. English is not my best subject and passing this drivers test is way more important, you know? Haa... (Beat, sneezes.) Ugh, allergies! I hate this... Allergies. I'm allergic to fresh cut grass, wheat, rabbits and sun dried tomatoes. (Sneeze) Excuse me. So, Mr. Brock told you about me? Ha! That's so funny. He's nice. Very specific. "Keep your hands on the wheel! Don't run that guy over! Oh my God we're gonna die!" He's so funny. I thought I would have definitely passed that time. I mean, after the third time, I just got angry, you know. Wasn't fair. They didn't put flags on the cones. That's just rude. (Beat) Oh, you're in charge of the cones? Really? Oh... I'm sorry. I ramble on and on when I'm nervous and stuff. It's just... Well, I'm on medication now and that's made all the difference, especially during games. Hand-eye coordination is way better and I don't stop and count the people in the crowd... And this year? I made varsity! Volleyball! Yeah, go team! Well that's mostly because Janet had that freak driving accident. A deer... and a clown... The deer lived. Yeah... I was in the car at the time of the, you know—crash, death trap, vehicular homicide, whatever. Oh, but I was not driving. No way, wasn't me. Nope. 'Cause if I was, the clown would have made it. Yeah, so, I'm taking her place on varsity, and my folks need me to drive myself home from practice so... Here I am. Again. And this time it's gonna happen! Seat belt, check! Fifth time is a charm! Get to go to all the varsity parties, stay out late... A varsity letter and a drivers license is a big step into coolness, you know, you get to do all the stuff you people got away with in the '60s but without the tie-dyes and armpit hair. Ha! Just joshin'. Ok! Mirrors, mirrors... Speaking of Janet, you know I can't help but notice that you have two broken arms. I know I shouldn't ask, but was it a bad driver? Your arms? Wait, no, no, don't answer that. 'Cause if it was, I don't want to bring up any bad memories... Like the ones I have of that clown... OMG, all that white paint left on the fender and that red nose swinging back and forth, and back and forth, and back and forth on the antenna.... So creepy. So sad. I can't go past a McDonald's without crying... I usually order a Happy Meal, but it's just not happy anymore... Anyway... Whoever wrote "suck me"—on both your casts—well, that is not a friend. So not a friend. (Aside). Rearview mirror... Check. Look behind me, check... This is so exciting. Don't you worry about a thing. I've been practicing! Oh, I guess I should start the car and back out, right? Ok. (Starts the car, smiles. She goes to back out but goes forward.) Ooops, ha. My B. Hehehe... That's so funny. (Sneeze) Ok, here we go...

The Speed of Sound

Who:

Whom:

When:

Where:

What:

Why:

How:

What:

How:

APPENDIX OF ACTIONS FOR ACTORS

Abuse	Enlist	Obliterate
Admonish	Ensnare	Overwhelm
Alarm	Entice	Pacify
Annihilate	Excite	Play
Amaze	Explain	Plead
Assert	Flatter	Prod
Bait	Flirt	Prove
Baffle	Frighten	Provoke
Blame	Hassle	Punish
Bribe	Help	Reassure
Bully	Hide	Reward
Cajole	Horrify	Save
Challenge	Humble	Scold
Chastise	Hurt	Seduce
Coax	Ignore	Shock
Complain	Impress	Show off
Crush	Incite	Soothe
Curse	Injure	Surprise
Dare	Intimidate	Taunt
Defend	Join	Tease
Deflate	Jolt	Threaten
Deny	Justify	Trick
Destroy	Lure	Torture
Devastate	Manipulate	Undermine
Educate	Mock	Upset
Encourage	Mother	Urge
Enlighten	Offend	Warn

ABOUT THE AUTHOR

Tia Dionne Hodge-Jones is an award-winning writer/play-wright, actor, and director/producer. As an actress, she has appeared in numerous national and regional on-camera and voice-over/radio commercials, and has appeared on *Law & Order, Law & Order*: *Criminal Intent, Conviction*, as well as the pilot, *The Third Degree*, for Fox. In 1998, she received a Best Actress nomination by the Independent Reviewers of New England for her per-formance as "Veronica" in New Repertory Theatre's pro-duction of Athol Fugard's *Valley Song*. More recently, she appeared as the recurring characters "Angel Mel" and "Amelia Bennett" on ABC's *One Life to Live*. She then played "Melanie Clarke" on 666 Park Avenue, and was a panelist on Cafemom.com's Coffee Shop Confessions. Her plays, *Puddin', Love... Like Lemonade* and *A Spider in Wine* all received workshops by New Jersey Dramatists & Waterfront Ensemble (Hoboken, NJ). Recently, *A Spider in Wine* was accepted into the Classical Theatre of Harlem's Playwrights Playground (NY, NY, 2014). *Puddin'*, was accepted into the New Perspectives Theatre Company Voices From the Edge 6.0 & 7.0 Festivals (NY, NY), was an alternate for the NY International Fringe Festival in 2003, and was accepted into the 2009 New Moon Reading Series at Luna Stage (Montclair, NJ,) and the 2009 NY International Fringe Festival.

Behind the camera, Tia Dionne wrote, produced and directed two short films for the inaugural NYC Midnight

Movie Madness Filmmaking Competition (2002), and was awarded the First Runner-up prize for *Once Upon A Once Upon*. In 2003, Tia Dionne associate produced *Crutch*; marking filmmaker Rob Moretti's directorial debut (HP Productions, LLC., in association with Illuminare Entertainment (Distribution) and Ardustry Entertainment.) Tia Dionne also directed and produced the pilot episode of *UnCorked: A Slightly Irreverent Look at Wine* for Wine Ventures, LLC, in association with Fulton Street Films. The project debuted at New Filmmakers Docs, Mocks & More in 2006, and was an Official Selection at MemFest (2006). *UnCorked* also garnered Tia Dionne a Directors Citation from the Black Maria Film Festival in the spring of 2007. She has since directed episodes for BN4REAL. TV, and has produced/directed live events and video projects for America Scores and Veterans Across America. Her pilot—*The Whiskey*—was an Official Selection at the Producers Guild of America Lab at the Sundance Film Festival (2009).

For more information about Tia Dionne's upcoming books, workshops, and projects, please visit www. TiaDionneHodge.com.

CPSIA information can be obtained
at www.ICGtesting.com
Printed in the USA
BVHW01s0222120218
507873BV00021B/401/P